Steve Boga

RISK!

An Exploration into the Lives of Athletes on the Edge

North Atlantic Books
Berkeley, California

Risk!
An Exploration into the Lives of Athletes on the Edge

Copyright© 1988 by Steve Boga

ISBN 1-55643-042-6

Published by North Atlantic Books
   2800 Woolsey Street
   Berkeley, California 94705

Cover photograph of Jon Lugbill by Catherine Summers
Cover and book design by Paula Morrison
Typeset by Campaigne and Somit Typography

Risk! is sponsored by the Society for the Study of Native Arts and Sciences, a nonprofit educational corporation whose goals are to develop an ecological and crosscultural perspective linking various scientific, social, and artistic fields; to nuture a holistic view of arts, sciences, humanities, and healing; and to publish and distribute literature on the relationship of mind, body, and nature.

Library of Congress Cataloging-in-Publication Data

Boga, Steve, 1947–
   Risk! / Steve Boga.
      p.   cm.
   ISBN 1-556-43042-6 : $9.95
   1. Athletes—Biography.   2. Risk taking (Psychology)   I. Title.
GV697.A1B557 1988
796'.092'2—dc19
   [B]   88-25590
                                                                        CIP

to Bruce Maxwell

CONTENTS

Introduction by Eric Heiden ix

Preface xi

Rock Star: John Bachar 1

River Rat: Jon Lugbill 17

Ironman: Dave Scott 33

Ultra-Marathoner: Ruth Anderson 47

King of the Road: Kenny Roberts 61

Mountain Medico: Peter Hackett 77

Winged Wonder: Jan Case 95

Misadventurer: Rick Sylvester 111

Pedal Pusher: John Howard 129

Speed Freak: Steve McKinney 145

INTRODUCTION

There is a special kind of risk associated with sports in which the athlete has to work things out for himself. Whether it's the sports I've done—speed skating, bicycling—or the ones I've only admired from afar—rock climbing, motorcycle racing, whitewater canoeing—physical risk is just one of the obstacles to success. Besides the pain inherent in training long hours, and the risk of pulled muscles, broken bones or death, there is also the risk of failure. Individual sports force you to do it on your own. To perform well in a sport in which you know there is nobody else to rely on requires incredible mental toughness. As rock climber John Bachar says in the first profile, "It tweeks you mentally."

For me, there is nothing quite like going fast on a pair of skates. From the age of 14, I trained relentlessly—3 to 6 hours a day. I aspired to be as fast as I could be—and emerged an Olympic gold medalist. I would still love to glide over the ice at 40 mph, but I am no longer willing to commit the time and energy necessary to compete at the highest level—that is, at the level that satisfies me. In individual sports requiring extraordinary dedication and perseverance, the burnout rate is high.

I don't feel I've lost that dedication or perseverance—just redirected it toward becoming a doctor. My career as a sportsman has helped me tackle medical school. When I'm dog-tired and it doesn't seem like I'm ever going to get to the end, I know how to rely on myself.

That's why I so admire the accomplishments of the risk-athletes profiled in this book. People like John Bachar, Steve McKinney and my friend Dave Scott continue to compete, to confront the physical and mental risks, even though they have been at the top of their sports for years. They somehow possess a unique ability to reach deep within for that nugget of strength . . . then keep on reaching.

Eric Heiden

PREFACE

The seed of the idea for this book was planted one rainy Sunday afternoon while watching a videotape of a movie called "Heart Like A Wheel." It's the story of drag-racing queen Shirley "Cha-Cha" Muldowney, who overcame sexual prejudice and devastating injuries to twice become world champion. As I watched her explode from the starting line in one of the fastest sports on earth, two questions kept popping into my head: (1) why?—as in why does someone go into such an "offbeat" sport? (2) what?—as in what skills are needed to become the best drag racer that ever lived?

I began to wonder if others, too, might be curious about the answers to those questions. The idea became a project. I set out to find and interview a world-class athlete in an unsung sport and, well, sing out about him. When the wristwrestling world championship came to town, I interviewed and profiled Cleve Dean, the 470-pound world champion in that sport. I enjoyed it so much, I decided to do it again. The project became a book. I interviewed the best bowler in the world, and had my sights set on the top badminton player, when it struck me that some crucial element was missing. To add the necessary emotional edge to the profiles, more was needed than just the fear of losing. What that was, I finally decided, was the fear of dying.

There is a story about a psychiatrist, new to the profession, who tells her rock-climbing patient how much she admires her fearlessness. The patient answers, "What makes you think I'm fearless? I'm just as scared as anyone else. Sometimes I tremble and cry all the way up a difficult pitch."

"Why do you keep doing it then?"

"I don't know. That's why I came to you—to find out."

The lesson here is not that Extreme Risk Takers (ERT's) are fearless, but that they have learned how to handle fear. For Yosemite climbers, the wall of El Capitan is a laboratory for learning about and controlling fear. Climbing teaches them that fear is an acceptable—even a useful—emotion. They learn that they can be frightened and still perform. As one of them said, "Fear becomes a familiar companion."

Most of the athletes profiled here are, or recently have been, at the very pinnacle of their sport. Still, I was confident they would talk to me. Unlike, say, John McEnroe who gets more media attention than he wants or deserves, former speed-skiing world-record holder Steve McKinney gets much less. He is one of only two men in the world who has skied more than 130 mph, yet how many know his name? On the other hand, his sister, Tamara McKinney, the first American woman to win the World Cup, can be seen promoting ski paraphernalia in glitzy periodicals. Maybe it's simply a matter of how often your sport is broadcast on TV.

I have often been asked how I chose the athletes. (The next question is usually something like, "Why didn't you choose George Willig?" ... "Or Robby Naish?" ... "Or my uncle Bart, who is really an amazing guy...?") Well, I picked the sports all right; but in some strange way I don't feel as if I chose the athletes at all. I decided on their qualifications—they had to be Alive, American, Available to be Interviewed, and Extreme Risk Takers —but then for the most part I just waited for excellence to shine forth. And shine forth it did. When you talk rock climbing with people in the know, the name "John Bachar" just keeps coming up. The same is true of Steve McKinney and Speed Skiing; Jon Lugbill and Canoeing; Kenny Roberts and Motorcycle Racing; and Dave Scott and Ironman Triathlons.

I sought sportsmen rather than stuntmen. Thus my rejection of Larry Walters, who flew a lawn chair suspended from 42 helium-filled weather balloons. (After reaching an altitude of 16,000 feet, Walters began popping the balloons with a pellet gun until he was able to land safely.) Thus, too, my choice of Yosemite Free Climber John Bachar over, say, stuntman George Willig, who attained meteoric fame by performing the first exterior ascent of the World Trade Center. A stunt.

Boardsailor Robby Naish was 11th on my list, a near miss, but the real choice in that sport, had he been American, would have been Baron Arnaud de Rosnay who once crossed the Bering Sea from the United States to the Soviet Union on a sailboard. Unfortunately, in

1984 Rosnay disqualified himself on a second count by disappearing while attempting to boardsail across the Strait of Taiwan.

There have been plenty of disqualifications by death, but for those who live to keep pushing the limits, the question is not so much "Why?" as "Why not?" Risk athletes see with their special vision the physical and psychological benefits they derive from their risk taking, and they can only wonder why everybody isn't out climbing rocks, paddling rivers, or skiing down mountains.

Many ERT's report feeling intense rushes of exhilaration, even euphoria, when they break through the risk barrier. As one ERT put it: "You've roared and cried and grunted your way up that impossible wall, then that last little scramble gets you to the top and you stand there yodeling."

And then there's Peter Bird, 36, a London-based photographer who tried to row solo from San Francisco to Australia. After 296 days of rowing 9,560 miles, he got stranded on the Great Barrier Reef. When the rescuers asked him why he'd done it, he answered, "It's an adventure. You don't have to justify it. It's just an adventure."

"Jumping is like a knife cutting through the malarkey of life."

—Carl Boenish

"A good scare is worth more to a man than good advice."

—Ed Howe

ROCK STAR

> " ... No man can completely summon all his strength, all his will, all his energy, for the last desperate move, till he is convinced the last bridge is down behind him and that there is nowhere to go but on."
> —Heinrich Harrer

On a soon-to-be-hot September morning in Yosemite Valley, free soloist John Bachar laces on his climbing boots and stares intently at the sheer granite wall that towers before him. He closes his eyes and pictures himself climbing one of its 250-foot vertical routes, the one called "Crack-A-Go-Go". Its polished surface is marred only by a few tiny irregularities and two dime-thin vertical cracks.

The difference between Bachar and countless souls who have preceded him is that after Bachar is finished picturing himself climbing Crack-A-Go-Go, he'll do it. He's done it before, maybe 100 times. Alone. Without ropes or hardware or the old-fashioned camaraderie of a partner. What he does is called free soloing, and he's the best in the world at it.

He straps on his equipment: a bag of grip-enhancing gymnastic chalk and his tight-fitting rock-climbing boots. That's all. That and a lot of courage, talent and determination.

He stands and stretches, not stiffly but slowly, carefully. Wearing only baggy white shorts and no shirt, he has a body worthy of one of the world's best rock climbers. Tanned from countless hours on the rock, it ripples with definition. Although listed as 5′

11″ and 160 pounds, he appears smaller, almost thin. He carries no excess weight, for, as everyone agrees, John Bachar travels light.

Slowly, with the grace of a lynx, he moves to the rock. Reaching into his bag, he dusts his hands, turning them as white as a mime's. He places one hand, then the other, on the rock, his finger joints tensing, swelling to fill the crack. "Finger jam" in place, he lifts his right leg to hip-level, fitting his toe-tip onto a postage-stamp-sized depression in the rock. With less effort than most people expend getting out of bed, he lifts himself off the ground and onto the granite, moving from the horizontal world to the vertical—equally at home in both.

Rock climbing predates man's use of tools, but it wasn't until the 20th Century that climbing became a sport. Mountaineers climbed rocks only when they couldn't go around them, and then without relish. As equipment improved, making virtually every mountain in the world climbable, many mountaineers sought new challenges in rock climbing. Their focus shifted from the Destination to the Dance.

The revolutionary changes in climbing have come about once a decade:

In the 1940's came the nylon rope.
In the 1950's came the steel piton.
In the 1960's came the chockstone.
In the 1970's came John Bachar.

In the conventional sport of rock climbing, a two-member team is joined by a 150-foot lifeline. One partner climbs, placing in the protective hardware, while the other anchors to a rock and belays the first with nylon ropes. If a climber rests on—or pulls himself up by—his equipment, he is said to have climbed "aided." If he uses his equipment only as a safety net, he is said to have climbed "free." If he leaves behind his rope, hardware and partner, he is said to have "free soloed." And if he free solos an extremely difficult climb—say, a 5.11c, like Crack-A-Go-Go—he is said, in some circles, to be crazy or to have a death wish.

Bachar, who has heard it all, is not amused. "I don't even listen anymore," he says. "If they were saying something intelligent, I might worry. Actually, I'm a conservative climber. Yeah, chicken. I'm always operating way below my level of ability. That's what I call the cushion. I hate feeling like I'm thrashing around up there. If I can't do it with control, I'll back off. In my own mind, I'm really a chicken."

No one privy to what Bachar does on a rock will buy that, but the man climbs with such self-possession, in such harmony with the rock, that one is temporarily persuaded that he doesn't take risks. Like all great performers, he makes it look easy. It is, in fact, impossible to gauge the difficulty of a route merely by watching Bachar solo it.

But no risks?

"Look at the things I don't do," he says. "I don't climb frozen waterfalls. Or crumbly rock. In Yosemite, it's solid rock, good weather. And the more I do it, the better I get. The odds are always with me."

According to Bachar, free soloing is the most popular participant sport in the world. "Everybody free solos. When you walk to the store, you're free soloing. It's just a matter of the difficulty of the route."

In the Yosemite decimal system, routes are classified as follows:

Class 1: a walk.

Class 2: proper footware required. ("Of course, that's ridiculous," says Bachar, "because the Nepalese go barefoot everywhere.")

Class 3: ropes advised, not because the climb is so difficult, but because a fall would be fatal.

Class 4: everyone—except free soloists—use ropes.

Class 5.0 to 5.14: the heart of the matter for most climbers. Bachar, however, won't sniff at anything less than 5.10. (For the few climbers who share his rarefied air, the most difficult climbs have been further delineated, as in 5.11a, 5.11b, 5.11c.)

Bachar, already 100 feet up Crack-A-Go-Go, is spread-eagled on the rock like a spider. His toes are jammed into such tiny holds that, from the base of the rock, the entire outline of the sole of his boot is visible.

Forty feet away, on a different route of the same rock, a German couple is climbing in the more conventional manner. Although they are "free climbing," they are heavily attired and laden with rope bandoliers and loops of hardware. Next to the half-naked Bachar, they appear otherworldly; next to them, Bachar's approach to climbing seems absurdly clean and simple.

When the German man finally spots Bachar, he stares, trans-
fixed. He calls down to his partner, who is still on the ground,
belaying him: " ... Solo?"

"Ja. Solo."

The woman, also intrigued, snaps several pictures of Bachar.
When two American climbers arrive at the base of the rock, she calls
over to them in a heavy accent: "Excuse me. Do you know the name
of this climber?"

"That's John Bachar."

Eyes light up in recognition. "Oh. Ja. Okay then."

Meanwhile, 150 feet above the Valley floor, with a straight drop
to his starting point, Bachar ponders his next move. After studying
the problem for a moment, he dusts his right hand with chalk and
forces it into a crack in the rock. Called a "hand-jam," the hold is
brutally painful to the ordinary mortal. But Bachar has extraordinary strength in his palm and finger muscles, the product of countless hours of exercising; by flexing those muscles, his hand expands
to fill the crack, creating a pivot-point so secure that it allows him to
lean away from the rock while he dusts his free hand. That accomplished, he lifts his foot to hip-level, setting it in a small depression in
the granite. Then, with a gentle lift, a fluid ease, he moves up the
rock.

Mr. and Mrs. Bachar didn't raise their son to be a rock climber. It was
assumed that John would follow his father and become a math whiz.
It sounded all right to John, who played along with straight A's in
high-school math. Meanwhile, he was also an athlete, playing baseball, then giving that up for pole vaulting. "I tied the school record in
practice," he remembers. "I dug vaulting. But by then I had discovered climbing. I started going to a climbing spot north of L.A.,
called Stony Point. By the time I was 16, I could do all the bouldering
problems there, something nobody else could claim."

By his senior year, he was cutting track practice to go climbing.
"I started out cutting Wednesdays, which, with the weekend, gave me
three days to climb. But it wasn't enough, so I started cutting Tues-
days and Thursdays, too...."

Because few could climb with John Bachar, he learned to climb
alone. "I didn't have any friends in high school," he says with a trace
of sadness. "I met a few people climbing—including Ron Kauk."

Kauk and Bachar were compatible on and off the rock. They were several levels better than anyone else, as though they played in a league all their own. When summer ended, Kauk coaxed Bachar to go to Yosemite with him, regaling him with stories of the Valley, "home of the best rock climbing in the world." But Bachar, not yet able to see the light, enrolled in math at U.C.L.A. Kauk dropped out of high school, moved to Yosemite and began free climbing new routes, making a name for himself.

During his freshman year, a distracted Bachar got a C in math. He was depressed and realized he had to get out of L.A. Most of the rock he'd seen in the last few months was in Japanese Tea Gardens. And Kauk's letters from Yosemite created a yearning he'd never felt before. "It is the best in the world!" he wrote. "Granite spires reaching for a blue sky, all waiting to be climbed by you and me. When you do a new route in Yosemite you get to name it. I've got thirteen already...."

John, anguished, sought advice. His mother, with whom he had lived since his parents split up 10 years before, had learned a thing or two about life. "Do what you love to do," she counseled, and the next day he quit U.C.L.A. and went to study in Yosemite. "It was a very big decision," he recalls. "My father was a research mathematician, a respected professor, and it was chiseled in the family rock that I should follow that route. He understood athletics all right—he'd played pro baseball—but he didn't understand giving up college for climbing. Now he digs it, seeing my name in all the magazines...."

Bachar moved to Yosemite and set up a permanent residence in Camp 4, the climbers' campground. Quickly, he and Kauk rose to the top rung in the rock climbing ladder. Bachar studied kinesiology and set up an outdoor gym in the middle of Camp 4 to work on certain muscle groups. They worked out together, climbed together and partied together, competing in all three. Comparing their progress, Kauk was forced to conclude that Bachar had it all: physical talent, discipline, fine analytical powers. Kauk was physically talented, and he was willing to work hard, but he lacked Bachar's ability to tear a problem apart and look at all its parts. Like a grand master chess player, Bachar could see many moves ahead, a skill he figured he inherited from his analytical father. "He gave me a logical way of thinking," says Bachar. "It's made me a more thorough thinker."

When he was 19, Bachar became the first person to free solo a

5.11 climb—Yosemite's 400-foot New Dimensions. It was a climb that had severely tested the mettle of the world's best two-man teams, and when word reached Camp 4 that Bachar had free soloed it, the other climbers were stunned. The following day, a notice appeared on the camp bulletin board: "Tell Webster to change the meaning of insanity to 'John Bachar free soloing New Dimensions!'"

Bachar remembers the furor. "I didn't tell anybody. Word just spread, but it was weird—nobody would talk to me about it. I could hear them whispering behind my back: 'There goes John Bachar ... he soloed New Dimensions.' Nobody understood it."

It didn't get any easier for Bachar. He further ostracized himself when he became the only person to solo a 5.11c route called Nabisco Wall, which had recently been listed in the Guiness as the world's most difficult roped climb. Then he did an "on-sight" (unpracticed and unrehearsed) free solo of Moratorium, a 5.11b and, as such, the hardest on-sight free solo ever. "On-sight is really the big leagues," says Bachar. "Not knowing what's up there makes all the difference in the world. Climbing Moratorium, I got too close to my limits and it didn't feel good. I didn't have that extra padding of security. I've only had a bad feeling on a couple of solos, but that was one of them."

Competitive tension between Kauk and Bachar intensified when Bachar was asked to do a TV commercial for 7-Up. It escalated when Bachar discovered that an obscure Spanish climbing boot, the Fire (pronounced "Fee-Ray") was far superior on Yosemite rock and started the Sole Survivor Corporation to exclusively import the boot. The last straw was Bachar installing himself as vice president in charge of testing the boots (i.e. climbing in them), for which he was paid a salary of $60,000.

Says Bachar: "The jealousy among climbers is intense. I wasn't living in Camp 4 and eating beans anymore. I wasn't one of the boys. For the first time in my life I had to file a 1040 form. A lot of climbers were asking, 'If he can do it, why can't I?' It got so bad between Kauk and me that one day he took offense at something he thought I said and began to slap me around. He was daring me to fight him. There was a time when I would have taken him up on it, but I guess I'd matured. I could see Ron had problems. Our relationship has gone downhill since then.

"Sometimes I wonder why I ever wanted any notoriety. In

climbing everybody is watching every little thing you do; then it gets reported and blown out of proportion. At times I feel like I don't have any friends. A lot of guys want to be number one so bad, they'll sacrifice any friendship for it. It's sad. I'm competitive, sure, but it doesn't drive me nuts. There are only two guys in the world who have impressed me with their climbing ability—Jerry Moffatt and Ron Kauk—and on certain days they can do things with their bodies that I can't do, and vice versa. That's all right, I learn from that. So many guys burn out and quit—they can't love the sport very much if they quit so easily, can they?"

Bachar certainly loves it. He intends to climb until he dies, and while the force raging within him is much more a life wish than a death wish, he willingly accepts the possibility of the end coming while he is climbing in what he calls Zone 3, which means quite simply, "If you fall, you die."

"Better there than in some dumb car accident," he says.

Saying that free soloing is John Bachar's specialty is like saying that ballet is Rudolph Nureyev's specialty. It does not go nearly far enough, for it is not just what the man does, but what he is. And no climber does it—or is it—better than Bachar. Without ropes, he climbs routes that 99% of the world's climbers wouldn't tackle with ropes. He is to most of the Camp 4 climbers as they are to a stone-cold novice.

Such domination probably exists in no other sport, yet Bachar receives no income directly from climbing. There are few formal competitions—most free-spirited climbers would find them ridiculous—and thus little prize money. The sport, relatively staid for today's television market, generates few endorsements; however, Bachar, with his beach-blond good looks, recently garnered an "Essence of Shaving" ad, which earned him in excess of $10,000.

"I didn't have to do anything really stupid," Bachar says, "like climb through a mountain of shaving cream. But they wanted me to wear a helmet." He grimaces at their naivete. "Nobody in Yosemite wears a helmet. Then they didn't like my voice and dubbed in somebody else. At least they let me free solo." Bachar has also appeared on "That's Incredible," "Real People" and "Evening Magazine." He finished third in a "Survival of the Fittest" contest, earning $5,000 and wiping out the competition in the Stick Fighting event. "It took place on a swinging bridge," he remembers. "Most of the other guys couldn't even walk across it. I could jog across it. I do well in the balance tests."

Sometimes the movies call him for stunt work. "They come to me," he says. "I give them my price and tell them to take it or leave it. They pay well, but I don't need money. I need rock."

One is inclined to believe him, for Bachar appears not to have a materialistic bone in his body. After 6 years of living in a tent or a van, he has moved into an unpretentious cabin in Yosemite with his wife, Brenda. The couple owns little. John's one concession to a five-figure income is his black Toyota 4-Runner, into the back of which he can pile the tools of his trade: boots, weights, ropes, chalk, bicycle. He can often be seen driving around the Valley, moving from one climb to another, less circumspect behind the wheel than on the rock, a Peter Tosh tape blaring from the car stereo.

Less than fifteen minutes after he began, Bachar is 250 feet up Crack-A-Go-Go, poised to go over the top. Nearby, the German woman struggles on the wall, fifteen feet off the ground. Although the Germans are accomplished climbers, they are tortoises to Bachar's hare. He will require one-tenth the time they will. Yet Bachar claims that speed is not his main concern; rather it is a byproduct of his perfect solo technique. "The summit is definitely secondary to me. I don't know about other people, but for me it's the dance that's important. The quality of the movements, like in Tai Chi. Or diving off a 10-meter board. Lots of people can dive from that high, but how many can do it with grace and control?"

Nevertheless, there is ample evidence that Bachar is proud of his quickness. "Some mornings I'll do Crack-A-Go-Go and Hardd (another 5.11), then go down to Arch Rock and do New Dimensions. When I come back, the roped climbers are still on their first climb. It saves a lot of time not having to put in and take out hardware."

One particular Yosemite climb offers evidence of just how segregated Bachar is from the climbing masses. The guide books say that Fairview Dome, a 1200-foot vertical ascent at Tuolumne Meadows is a 5–8 hour round trip for a roped party of two. Bachar, who uses it as a workout, has done it base to summit— 1200'—in 17 minutes.

Incredibly, he has also climbed El Capitan and Half Dome in the same day. Bachar explains: "Peter Croft and I started at the base of

El Capitan at midnight. Using no fixed ropes, we arrived at the top at 10:05 a.m., passing four parties who were spending two or three nights each! We ran down and arrived at the car at 11:10 a.m. Then we started hiking up to the base of Half Dome, arriving there at 1:20 p.m. We started climbing Half Dome at exactly 2:00 p.m., passed seven parties all of whom were going to spend the night on the wall, and topped out at 6:03 p.m., with two hours of light left. Total time from the base of El Capitan to the top of Hald Dome: 18:03. A killer day!"

The way some keep score in climbing is to count "first ascents," but Bachar isn't even sure how many he has. "About a hundred in Yosemite, I guess. That's not all that many, but they've all been fairly difficult."

The willingness of climbers to flout gravity has led them into inevitable conflict with the Park Service, which is responsible for retrieving the battered bodies of the fallen. Of the 100 or so Search and Rescue missions in Yosemite each year, at least 20 involve climbers. To the park rangers, free soloists like John Bachar are the lunatic fringe of an already ticky sport. To the freewheeling climbers, rangers are mainstream Establishment, wilderness cops; as such, they are viewed with the same sort of disdain shown, say, a climber who tackles a boulder with ropes.

Bachar's relationship with the rangers is more aloof than tense. "They think I'm crazy, but they can't stop me from doing what I'm doing," he says, with rising inflection. "They've stopped people from hang gliding and parachuting off El Cap, from kayaking the Merced River ... but they can't stop me."

One pictures John Bachar, in tights and cape, leaping from rock to rock, laughing in the face of the law. Except that laughing doesn't come easily to Bachar. Still, he has had a smile or two at the expense of the rangers. He recalls the time he had to convince one at Big Rock, in Southern California, that he was adequately equipped to climb in the park. Showing him a spatula, he told him it was a "crack-jack," an important climbing tool. He was waved through before he could produce his "inverted storm detector," a garden fork.

Yosemite's former chief ranger, Bill Wendt, found little humor in the park's relations with climbers. It was difficult not to think of them as, well, riffraff. After all, they caused more than their share of problems, from shoplifting in the Village store to falling off mountains. But Wendt was concerned with more than the welfare of a few climbers who were a burr in the side of the Park Service. He worried about the dangerous example they set for others. He once halted a television shoot of Bachar and Kauk until assurances were given that the program would carry a safety message. "It's too easy to copy someone on TV," he said. "Anyone attempting to free solo should realize that Bachar and Kauk are at the Olympic level."

Does Bachar worry about leading, by example, the novitiate climber to his doom? "No way. Free soloing has a built-in safety device. Someone who doesn't know what he's doing isn't going to get very far up a 5.11 climb. It's not going to happen. The novice will drop out long before Zone 3."

Climbing statistics support such a contention. Of the approximately 850 mountaineering and rock climbing fatalities in the United States from 1951 to 1984, only one was the result of a free-solo rock-climbing fall.

Others have come close. Bachar's pal, Rick Cashner, has twice fallen more than 30 feet and lived. "The average climber will die if he falls more than 47 feet," Bachar explains. "But 30 feet can do a lot of damage. Rick's a tough guy. He's broken a few bones, lost a few teeth, but he's still a climber. That's the way it is—real climbers do it for life. The second time Rick fell, he knocked out his front teeth and gashed his eyebrow pretty bad. A ranger scrambled up to him and found blood spurting from his brow. He thought it was coming from his eye and fainted, hitting his head on a rock and knocking himself out. So Rick had to hike out to get help for the ranger. Like I said, he's a tough guy."

Bachar himself has taken only one serious fall. On a difficult solo in Colorado's Eldorado Springs Canyon, he tumbled 20 feet. His amazing balance allowed him to land right-side up, but a dislodged rock knocked him down, badly bruising his back. After standing up, Bachar fainted, then revived and drove himself home. He, too, is a tough guy.

But even tough guys possess a realistic fear of falling. For climbers—particularly free soloists—it comes with the territory. The irony is that the fear itself—a supposedly self-protective emotion—can disrupt concentration and short-circuit skill. A climber can die as a direct result of being afraid to die.

How does Bachar deal with the fear?

"It forces me to concentrate. I zoom right in. But it's a relaxed sort of concentration. I get so into doing each movement—with grace and control—that it makes no difference whether I'm fifty feet up or five. If I think about falling, I can't put all my energy into doing the moves.

"You hear people say you shouldn't look down, but I look down all the time. I dig it. It's beautiful up there." Bachar reflects a moment. "People are obsessed with the dangers of soloing, but what they don't realize is that just about every move is reversible. If it's too hard, I can undo it. That's not the case with, say, speed skiing or hang gliding. In those sports, once you've started, you're committed.

"I accept the consequences of all that I do," he adds. "No matter what we do with our lives, our bodies are temporary. We're all going to die, and I'd rather die climbing than doing anything else."

For John Bachar, a shy smile is usually maximum evidence of amusement. He displays that smile, and his remarkable attitude toward falling, whenever he is asked for a climbing anecdote: "A guy was doing Reed's Direct, a 5.9 climb here in Yosemite. Not only was he tied in, but he had a drag line for hauling up equipment. From 150 feet up, he fell. But he had tied into his harness wrong and the rope ripped apart the harness, and now he's doing the death fall. He's history, except that his drag line wrapped around a tree on the wall, caught, and stopped him five feet from the ground." Again there is that shy smile. "He was doing the death fall and he lucked out. Most people don't even have a drag line on that climb. After that, he sold all his equipment and quit climbing. That one is pretty funny...."

One of climbing's main attractions is the exhilarating freedom it offers its participants. As there is no rule book, a climber is allowed to ascend a route employing any or all of the available hardware— unless, of course, he wants the respect of John Bachar.

"Someone says they did this 5.11a or that 5.11c, but how do you know? They write into an editor of some climbing magazine, what does that prove? Besides, with artificial aid, anybody can climb anything. It's about as challenging, as meaningful, as a repairman going up a telephone pole."

It's impossible to talk climbing with Bachar without talking ethics. For him, the two are inseparable. "Only in the last fifteen years have climbers quit a route because it couldn't be done unaided. In the past, if that happened, the party would just bolt up and go for the summit. Now the real purists figure if it can't be done right, it shouldn't be done at all."

Count Bachar among the real purists. A few years back he was invited to a climbing conference in Germany, one purpose of which was to discuss the ethics of climbing. "I thought it was going to be great," he says, shaking his head in disgust. "They paid my way there, which is unheard of. They had over 5,000 people in attendance, which is also unheard of. Here we'd have maybe 500. In Europe, climbers are revered as stars. In America I never get asked for my autograph, but the first day in Germany I signed about 300. Unfortunately, the discussions on ethics turned out to be bogus bullshit. They're just missing the point. They see nothing wrong with starting out at the top and putting in protection so you can climb safely from the bottom. Seems to me that's like getting a copy of the final exam before the exam."

Bachar's standards, as high as the walls he climbs, force him to question even his own methods. "I'm not as free as I could be," he says shamefully. "I use boots and chalk. If I was truly one with the rock, I'd use neither. But the chalk is organic; and climbing barefoot thrashes your feet ... " Again there is a hint of that smile. " ... and I'm not into pain."

Returning from the top of Crack-A-Go-Go, Bachar scampers down a dirt trail next to the rock, displaying his characteristic grace and coordination. He removes his climbing boots and puts on his beat-up Nike tennis shoes. Carrying his boots in one hand and his pouch of chalk in the other, he walks back to his car, taking a route dominated by huge slippery granite boulders. In love with the world he inhabits, he prances over the rocks.

Thirty minutes later, after a short lunch break of grapes and an apple, he is in Camp 4, staring at quite a different boulder. Thirty feet high, it has a name—"Midnight Lightning"—a "problem" (bouldering, a legitimate rock climbing subsport, calls its challenges "problems"), and a history. For years, climbers passed beneath its overhang, dismissing it as unclimbable; but in the mid-Seventies a denizen of Camp 4, his acuity sharpened by LSD, declared that he could see a solution. His vision was received as divine revelation in Camp 4, and some of the world's best climbers came to try to solve the problem of Midnight Lightning. Although that was more than a decade ago, only seven have succeeded. Ron Kauk was the first, John Bachar the second. Bachar has continued to do it as a regular part of his workout. "I've probably done Midnight Lightning 300 times."

Not today, however. This time, the "steel hooks" weaken, the hand slips and he drops ten feet, landing on the ground with a surprisingly heavy thud. Surprising because, up to then, he had seemed lighter than air. He sits for a moment, collecting his breath, contemplating his mistake. Finally he gets to his feet, saying, "First time I've fallen on this one in over a month. That's enough for today ... I'll finish the workout at the gym...."

Bachar's workout, which he does four days a week, is so strenuous that most people can't bear to watch him go through it. First, 2–3 hours soloing 5.11 climbs; then bouldering behind Camp 4 for a couple of hours, usually finishing with an assault on Midnight Lightning; then exercising in his outdoor gymnasium until dark.

"I built the gym myself in Rick Cashner's backyard when the one in Camp 4 became too much of a tourist trap. It got to the point that crowds were gathering just to watch me work out. Guys smoking cigarettes ... it drove me crazy. Most people would rather watch somebody else work out than work out themselves."

Among the gear Bachar has rigged there is a 2″ x 8″ board nailed between two pine trees. Attached to the board are tiny blocks of wood that provide tiny holds for one-armed fingertip pullups. The Guiness Book of World Records says that only one person in 100,000 can do a one-armed pull up. Bachar regularly does one-armed fingertip pullups—with barbell weights dangling from a harness around his waist!

"I do more than is necessary," he says, in between breaths. "That's my cushion. I want to be stronger than I'll ever need up on the rock. It's not just making it to the top; it's making it with control. There's no satisfaction in thrashing around and just barely making it. You can fool other people, but you can't fool yourself."

Bachar wants to be stronger, and better balanced. After several sets of pullups, he moves over to his "slack chain," which is strung between two trees. He hops up on the chain and proceeds to tiptoe from one end to the other, like a deft tightrope walker. "Besides balance, the chain tests concentration and relaxation," he says. "You gotta relax or it will throw you around."

Next he moves to the "crack machine," a long board with a built-in slot, for practicing "hand jams." Then back for more pullups.

"The only people who really do one-armed pullups are climbers. They aren't very good pressers, but they're usually great pullers. There are plenty of climbers who are stronger than me in the gym, but they can't always do it on the rock. Strength isn't everything. There's a woman here in Yosemite, one of the five best female climbers in the world. Not particularly strong, but great at solving climbing problems."

Working from power to endurance, Bachar moves to another piece of equipment, a personal invention of his called the Bachar Ladder. Tied to the top of a tree, it is a 70-foot modified rope ladder, which he climbs without the use of his feet. "I call it a rope ladder, but elsewhere they call it a Bachar Ladder," he says, tying a belay line around his waist. "It's funny. Where you live, they're jealous and don't want to call anything after you. In other places, they idolize you and name everything after you."

With a soft, determined hand-over-hand pull, Bachar glides to the top of the ladder. Without the use of his feet, he must utilize his tremendous upper-body strength. Though he never thrashes about or appears to struggle, his bulging back and shoulder muscles indicate maximum exertion.

Back down on the ground, in the lengthening shadows of the forest, Bachar puts on a T-shirt that reads "Damn The Rules, It's The Feeling That Counts," beneath a picture of a man playing a saxophone.

"John Coltrane," he explains, identifying the man on the sax. "One of my heroes. He was so dedicated, he used to practice eight hours a day, then go play gigs at night. He once lived in a place where he couldn't make noise, so he'd blow silent scales for two hours at a time. Dedication, I admire that...."

Bachar recalls an article on him wherein the author referred to John as "The Babe Ruth of climbing." "I didn't like that very much," he says. "Ruth had talent, but he wasn't very dedicated. I would have preferred 'The Marvin Haglar of climbing'. Or maybe 'The Bruce Lee'. Yeah, or John Coltrane."

Bachar has played the saxophone for years, and it is rumored that he plays it while driving. "Only on the straightaways," he says, smiling uninhibitedly now. "When I go to L.A. on business, I'll put on a jazz tape, steer with my knees and jam to the music."

In his gym, Bachar straps a watch around a conventional pullup bar. Then he clips a 20-pound weight to the harness belt that he wears. It dangles in front of him, suggestive of some medieval torture. For the next twenty minutes, he does sets of three one-armed pullups, resting a minute in between sets.

"You hear a lot now about the 'Type T' personalities of the people doing risk sports. Supposedly these Type T's get off on danger. I don't buy it. They may start climbing because of the danger, but real climbers won't stay with it for that reason. We have a saying: 'There are old climbers and there are bold climbers, but there are no old bold climbers.' I think people do the so-called risk sports because they find their jobs aren't physically demanding. So they get out and climb a rock."

In preparation for his next set of pullups, Bachar closes his eyes and steadies his breathing. "I practice mental imagery while I'm working out," he says. "That way I can use it on the rock, when it really matters. I might pretend that a light switch has suddenly been turned on and that electricity is surging through me and there's nothing anybody can do to stop it. It works great for a two-second move."

At other times, Bachar imagines that his fingers are steel hooks, and given his prodigious displays of strength, he must have an excellent imagination. *People Magazine* ran a picture of Bachar that caused their readers to gasp collectively. He is doing a one-armed hang from a rock ledge, high over oblivion. "That was a pretty big ledge," he says. "I can hang from something like that for over a minute anyway."

But the sport, he insists, is as much mental as physical. "Take that slack chain. Lots of people could walk back and forth on it when it's only two feet off the ground. But put it 100 feet up and see what happens. It's the same physical event, but it tweeks you mentally to be that high without protection."

Unquestionably, Bachar has great physical ability—the required strength and balance—and he works harder than anybody else to stay in shape. But he feels his real advantage over others is from the neck up. Mental toughness. The ability to concentrate during gripping situations.

"You have to be able to look at a climbing problem logically, dispassionately. Up on the rock, you don't get textbook situations. You need to be able to stay cool and improvise. Pre-visualization. I can look ahead and see that certain moves aren't going to work. A knowledge of the body is helpful, but even more important is an intuitive feeling for what it can do in tough situations."

It makes sense that John Bachar is a great rock climber, because he loves it so much. When he talks about it, he is uncharacteristically animated. You get the feeling that hardly anyone has ever loved a thing as much as Bachar loves climbing. "It's goddamn great," he effuses. "I can't understand why people play baseball when they could be climbing. It's so many things, not just one. Outdoors ... beautiful, with unbelievable exposures ... mentally challenging ... gives you the chance to face fear and overcome it....And it's so natural ... little boys are always climbing trees, aren't they? ... But the real reward is being able to look within, to learn about myself. It's a transient thing, that's why I keep going back up the rock—to relearn it.

"I don't have a list of goals. I'm like a dancer working on his dance. It may seem like I'm doing the same thing over and over, but each time it's a new experience. Each time I'll be more in control, more efficient, more artistic...."

But what about the approval of the fans? What about the cheers of the crowd that greet other great sportsmen when they finish their event? Doesn't Bachar miss the sound of applause?

As he removes the harness from his waist, his lips widen to a smile. Then a laugh. "Ha!" he cries. "I'd rather hear the wind."

RIVER RAT

"Man is the measure of all things."
                                    —Protagoras (fifth century B. C.)

ISERE RIVER, FRANCE, JULY 9, 1987: Twenty minutes before the start of his second slalom run at the Whitewater World Championships, Jon Lugbill wriggles into the tiny crawlspace of his sleek Kevlar C1 racer and begins a couple of minutes of stretching and easy paddling. He follows that with 6 or 7 minutes of what he calls "paddling pretty hard"—what most people would call "paddling very hard." It's enough to raise his pulse to about 110, a level he maintains for a few moments. From the waist down he is protected by a neoprene spray skirt attached to the cockpit, and the impression is one of a man with no legs at all. One sees torso, head and boat bobbing and weaving as one fluid form. After awhile he stops and floats. Oblivious to the cold drizzle, he closes his eyes and lets a river of tension flow from him.

He pictures the 600-meter slalom course before him. It is not a precise visualization, for he has already gone over that many times. This time he divides the course into segments, attaching a key word or phrase to each segment: First, "gun it!" ... second, "nice and easy" ... third, "stern pivot".... At the starting gate, aides hold his boat two meters behind the electric eye. He snaps on the chin strap of his helmet and rhythmically fingers the throat of his paddle. His concentration is total now, his mind firmly in control of the events. He has prepared himself to do the best he can do this day—all day. Even if his first run holds up as the winner, he will not be satisfied unless he improves his time on his second run. He is thinking positively, but cautiously. Mostly, he knows, he must guard against being too "up"; for with all the hype that surrounds the World Championships, it's easy to let adrenalin dominate and ignore the finesse demands of the sport. In order to calm himself, he thinks of past victories ... of a beautiful day at the beach. . . .

Jon Lugbill, 26, of Brookmont, a suburb of Bethesda, Maryland, is the greatest whitewater canoeist ever. He is undefeated in four of the last 5 biennial World Championships, winning the C1 class in both the individual and team events for a total of nine gold medals, more than anyone in canoe-slalom history.

Lugbill, like all C1-class racers uses a one-man, covered canoe that looks like a kayak, but requires a more sophisticated technique. Canoeists use a single-blade paddle and must kneel, whereas kayakers use a double-blade paddle and sit. Says Jon: "Someone who has never done either sport is more likely to take up the kayak because it's simpler to learn: The canoe is harder to maneuver and requires a lot more power because you're only doing about half the strokes. You also have to learn to balance with only one blade on one side."

Lugbill is 5'9" and 175 pounds, with brown wavy hair and a shy, self-effacing smile that immediately puts people at ease. Rock hard, he has huge shoulders, and muscular but proportionally smaller legs. "Usually I bicycle to work (he is an environmental scientist working on water quality issues on the Potomac), but about six weeks before the Worlds, I start to get real specific with my sport. I purposefully work for an imbalance. One time I met George Murray, the great wheelchair marathoner. We hit it off really well, had a lot in common—like, neither of us use our legs in our respective sports." There is, however, ample evidence that Lugbill does use his feet. He sports fleshy tumor-like protrusions on the tops of his feet, the result of daily rubbing against boat bottoms. They suggest killer bee stings.

For Jon Lugbill, canoeing has long been a family affair. The Lugbills were introduced to it in 1971, when Jon was ten years old. His father, Ralph, and the three Lugbill sons traveled to Petersburg, West Virginia, to attend a race of "Anything That Floats."

They collected about thirty inner tubes, laced them together and called it a raft. Race officials disqualified Jon and brother Ron because they were too young; so Ralph and number-one son, Kent, competed, finishing dead last.

Despite the defeat, the family had caught a Feeling. They were all fascinated by the whitewater exhibits, the carnival atmosphere of the competition, the jumble of boats and helmets and colorful gear. The following year, the family returned to Petersburg, where Ralph tried out a kayak, liked it and bought it. Later he bought a second boat, and the Lugbill's backyard began to take on the look of a used boat yard.

Ralph later became disenchanted with the kayak and bought a C-2, a two-person canoe. He and middle son, Ron, used it often. But until he was 14 Jon would suffer from Osgood Schlatter's, a disease in which the tendons grow too slowly to keep up with the bones; consequently, the kneeling demanded by canoes hurt his knees. For the time being, he would stay with kayaks.

When Jon was 12, he entered his first race, the Petersburg Wildwater Race. His first slalom was also that year, and he offers a terse analysis of that event. "The water was about 35 degrees. I swam twice. I finished last. It was miserable."

A year later he saw a paddler die. "The guy lost his boat. He was swimming and tried to walk out of the river," he explains. "He got caught under a submerged ledge, the current broke both his legs and he died. I've thought about why I wasn't more torn up. First of all I didn't know him; second, he had obviously been really stupid. Even then, I knew you didn't try to walk out of white water. If you didn't know how to roll, you floated downstream with your feet up. I guess I didn't really associate any risk with me."

As much as he hated losing, Lugbill hated doing it wrong. And floating downstream with legs flailing, he knew, was definitely wrong. The proper way to finish a race was in the boat. "I never swim anymore," says Jon. "If I go over, I roll. In white water, any time you swim, you're out of control. It's five times more dangerous whenever you leave your boat."

Jon and Ron convinced their parents to finance a trip to Colorado and a whitewater training camp for juniors. While their teen-aged peers were playing baseball and learning how to tie Boy Scout knots, the Lugbill kids were perfecting their paddling strokes.

"Colorado hardened us a lot," Jon says. "It was high-altitude white water that even today I'd call tough. We got hammered a lot. Before then we didn't know anything about hard white water. We just stayed away from it, figuring it was too dangerous."

Dangerous, but delightfully fun. For the Lugbill teenagers, that's what it was all about. "We weren't paddling to get good," Jon says, "we were paddling because it was fun." Their enthusiasm reached Ralph back home, and he and another father flew out to Colorado to see for themselves. The parents paddled a C-2 together and watched their sons catching onto something.

Back home in Brookmont, the Lugbill brothers set up a single slalom gate on a neighborhood pond no bigger than their garage, then paddled every day for the rest of the summer. Sometimes their Dad, ever-supportive, drove them to the Potomac to practice. They worked diligently to get a "bomb-proof roll," both left-side and right-side versions. "Only then," says Jon, "could we approach white water with the confidence needed to keep pushing the limits without fear."

By age 14, Jon was his adult size: a mesomorphic 5'9", 175 pounds. With his tendon problems behind him, he and Ron began training in the C-2. He admits that paddling a canoe became all the more attractive because for so long it had been denied him. That fall Ron and Jon entered their first C-2 competitions, placing fourth and fifth at the Savage and Youghiogheny races. The winter that followed was unusually warm and the boys were able to paddle straight through till spring.

They rigged three gates on their pond and intensified their workouts. At races they began to regularly attract remarks like "If you boys keep working at it, you just might make the U.S White-water Team." Enthusiasm fueled, they soon had ten gates on a part of the Potomac called Yellow Falls. Ralph would usually drive them to the river and then time them on their short runs. They were paddling 4-5 times a week now, half on the pond, half on the river.

Then in 1975, Ron, 16, and Jon, 14, qualified as the third American boat in the C-2 event at the White Water World Championships in Skopje, Yugoslavia. "We were in complete shock," says Jon. "We couldn't believe we had made the team. But talking to the other guys on the team, I was really disappointed in their attitudes. We found out these guys didn't paddle in the winter, or even in the fall.

They didn't seem to like it very much. They were just doing it to make the U.S. Team, but for some reason it didn't bother them that they were getting their butts kicked in Europe every two years."

Which is exactly what happened that year at Skopje. The Lugbill boat finished 22nd out of 26, but the brothers returned home convinced that if they combined proper training techniques with all the boat time they were putting in, they would improve. Or as Jon puts it: "We knew if we trained right, we'd blow those guys away."

Now they were paddling to get good as well as have fun.

ISERE RIVER: With a dramatic eruption of power, Jon Lugbill thrusts his paddle into the water; and with a frenzied succession of strokes, pivots the boat tight left past the electric eye and out into the current. He is quickly shrouded in the rapid's spume.

At gate #1, a downstream gate with fast, powerful water, he paddles on the backs of the waves to keep the bow up . . . then through the gate, keeping the boat in line for #2, which is in a flat, quiet eddy . . . beware the tendency to lose concentration, to come in too high . . . aim low now . . . ahh, perfect. . . .

Then through #2 . . . a pile of rocks creates tricky eddies . . . use the S-turn . . . perfect again. . . .

Canoes have been around a long time: Excavation of stone-age sites have yielded primitive canoes. Columbus called the dugout crafts of the Arawak Indians "canoas," which is the origin of the English word.

In 1867, George Waters of Troy, New York developed a laminated paper canoe, in which an intrepid Nathanial Bishop paddled 2,500 miles. By 1886 the America Canoeing Association was organized. And by 1900 canoeing was so popular that the city of Boston had a regular staff of Canoe Police to enforce proper morals among the canoeing public.

After World War II, the best canoes were made out of aluminum, which was inexpensive, lightweight and durable. With boats now available that didn't shatter or splinter on contact, whitewater canoeing became a sport in its own right; or rather several sports— with C-1 Slalom the glory event.

Slalom differs from other canoe competition in that it is a short (3-or-so minute) sprint through 25 pairs of poles—or gates—

suspended four feet apart and ten inches above fast-moving water. The gates, which suggest malnourished barber poles, may be run downstream (green-and-white striped) or upstream (red-and-white striped). The goal is to run "fast and clean"—that is, free of penalties. A running time is kept and there are 5-second penalties for touching a gate, 50-second penalties for missing one altogether. The final score is the better of two runs.

There are four classes in slalom racing: one-man canoes, or C-1; two-man canoes, C-2; one-man kayaks, K-1; one-woman kayaks, K-1w. Rule changes have narrowed the obvious differences between kayaks and canoes, so that today the two appear almost identical. Yet the fundamental difference between the two sports persists: The kayaker sits in his boat and uses a double-blade paddle, while the canoeist kneels and uses a single-blade paddle.

The first world championships were held in 1949 in Switzerland, and Europeans swept the medals—just as they would for the next thirty years. The Americans got into it in 1957, but most of the Yanks who made it to the finish line that year were not in their boats; and those who were had times near the bottom. Through the next ten biennial World Championships, the Americans remained the Rodney Dangerfields of whitewater slalom.

A decade later "TOP TEN IN '67" buttons were being sold to raise money for the team. Massachusetts paddler Barbara Wright responded to the prophesy with a career performance, finishing 9th out of 17 in the K-1W slalom.

Then in 1972, the West Germans added whitewater slalom events to the Olympic program. Jamie McEwan of Maryland pulled an epic upset, winning a bronze medal in the C-1 class before a huge TV audience that included impressionable 11-year-old Jonny Lugbill.

Bill Endicott, the U.S. Whitewater coach and an assistant at those '72 Olympics, says, "Jamie was a D.C. paddler, and his bronze medal had a tremendous effect on the sport in this country and this area. Before '72 the U.S. had never done anything worthwhile on the international level. When he finished third, all the kids saw it. They thought, 'If he can do it, maybe we can too.'"

With the advent of faster, lighter fiberglass boats, slalom times continued to drop. Throughout this period, the kayak class remained at the vanguard of slalom racing. One reason was an East German technique called "sneaking," in which a kayaker—with his flat-ended boat—could power out of an upstream gate as soon as his body had cleared the poles. With a lean here, a sweep-stroke there, an accomplished paddler could slip his back deck underneath the outside pole, shaving microseconds off his time. The C-1, with its upturned ends, could not keep up.

The Seventies saw a host of rule changes that spurred a C-1 uprising. In 1971 canoeists were permitted to reduce the minimum width of their C-1's from 80 cm. to 70 cm.—more in line with the kayak's 60 cm. minimum. Two years later the rules finally allowed canoes to be lower at the ends than the middle. Canoes no longer had to look like canoes; they could look like ... kayaks. It was the dawning of the age of canoe gate sneaking.

There began an off-river race to design a canoe that could take maximum advantage of the new rule changes. First, three D.C. paddlers came up with a revolutionary closed-cockpit C-2, called the Gemini. Then in 1977, Jon Lugbill, Bob Robison and Davey Hearn collaborated on the design of a canoe they called Max II, short for "To the Maximum," the group's rally cry. In the next few years they continued to make design improvements, resulting in sequels like Supermax, Ultramax, Cudamax and Batmax. The state-of-the-art Max was more maneuverable than the Roock-Schmidt, the leading European C-1, and it could "sneak" with the best kayaks. At the 1977 World Championships, Bob Robison finished fourth in C-1, by far the best American showing to date.

Two years later, in Jonquiere, Canada, the Americans swept the medals. The Jon Lugbill Era had arrived.

ISERE RIVER: ... through #3, a downstream gate on the right side, then sharp left, a combination move, avoid the eddies, lean left, right, left ... get the arm back quickly on recovery, short strokes, short and powerful, close the angle of the paddle just so, get the right exit angle, cross-current drive—watch out for the hole ... change the paddle angle and put on the brakes, change it again and turn upstream, pick up the stroke rate ... now "gun it," until the heart feels like it's going to leap through the chest....

A few miles upriver from the White House, the Potomac is a tumble of white water, presenting one of the most scenically dramatic obstacles to navigation in the U.S. George Washington, seeking to remove those obstacles, built five bypass canals to skirt the rapids and waterfalls: The idea, spawned in his youth, was for the river to one day carry the commerce of the new nation from the hinterlands to the marketplace. Today a half-mile remains of his Feeder Canal, a lush, overgrown habitat for dozens of varieties of animal and bird life. It is also the habitat for the U.S. Whitewater Team, whose members can be found there training year-round in fog, rain, snow or the gagging humidity of a Washington summer.

The paddler who can be found there most frequently is Jon Lugbill. The most significant person to ever find him: Bill Endicott, whitewater coach extraordinaire.

Tall, bespectacled, professorial-looking Bill Endicott appeared at a local slalom race one day in 1977 and announced that he wanted to do some coaching. People listened to him, for the man was not without credentials: He had rowed at Harvard (where he'd earned a master's degree in public administration). He had been a national paddling champion in C-2 and a member of the U.S. Whitewater Team. Lacking that "special something" required to be world-class, however, he dropped out of competitive paddling and went to work for several Washington congressmen. When one of them dropped prematurely dead from a heart attack, Endicott decided to get out, to seek a more physical life. When his father died and left him some money, it occurred to him that he could do whatever he wanted—namely coach and write books on whitewater racing.

When Endicott arrived at the Feeder Canal, he found a group of local kids—Jon and Ron Lugbill, Cathy and Davey Hearn, and others—paddling the Potomac during the coldest months of the year. That was to the average canoeist what a winter ascent of Mt. Everest was to the average climber. Calling themselves the Canoe Cruiser's Association, they were little more than a bunch of renegade kids having a blast in their boats. Endicott recognized the kids' talent and moxie, but he also recognized their lack of discipline. He convinced them they needed his talents in order to improve theirs.

Says Jon: "It was like before Bill we were a loose collection of boxcars. But when Bill became the engineer, he gave us real unity and direction."

Endicott brought his rigid training regimen to the Brookmont kids and they responded enthusiastically. He encouraged them to spend more time in their boats and less time lifting weights and running, all of which appealed to their natural instincts anyway. To drive the point across, he often said rhetorically, "Do runners train by paddling?" Once in their boats, he insisted, they should go all out, doing plenty of gate work, especially in rapids. And they should do timed, competitive runs over short courses. This, too, appealed to the Brookmont kids because, more than anything, they loved to go fast: But Endicott's advice flew in the face of the sports pundits, who had traditionally advised paddlers to train with longer runs at less than full speed. Endicott taught them that slalom paddling was essentially a series of power moves done again and again.

Jon Lugbill, who was still in high school when Endicott arrived, was not yet ready to devote himself monastically to paddling. Physically he was mature, a man-child who at 14 could bench-press 225 pounds. Throughout his high-school years, Lugbill continued to pump iron and play football, to the detriment of his paddling. Often he would arrive at the Feeder Canal black and blue from football practice, then have to squeeze himself into the cramped cubicle of his canoe and paddle hard for the duration of an Endicott training session.

When Lugbill speaks of his football experiences, he recalls the positives: "It kept me well-rounded athletically.... It taught me aggressiveness, discipline, and how to deal with pain." But when Endicott speaks of it, he tends to dwell on the negatives: "Jon did poorly in races in 1977-78 (his first two years of high school), a time of heavy weight training and football. To be a great paddler you have to practice the skills specific to the sport. There's no evidence of a carry-over from weight lifting to paddling."

Midway through high school, Lugbill began devoting himself with increased intensity to the pursuit of the C-1 World Championship. His talent and dedication—plus the synergistic impact of great coach and great paddler—brought results.

Endicott began to spend lots of individual time with Lugbill. He couldn't teach him much about "fast," but he had lots to show him about "clean." He taught him how to back off, how to temper his aggressiveness with technique. That, of course, ran counter to Lugbill's guts-out nature, and he resisted.

In the spring races of the 1978 season, when Lugbill was still in high school, he had times that rivaled those of the fastest kayaks. But he was still blowing big leads and losing races he should have won:

He vowed to prove he was no "choker."

ISERE RIVER: At gate #15, coming out of a tough angled upstream gate, very fast with lots of lean ... done everything right so far ... feeling good and confident, but have to keep up the concentration ... now's the time to hammer down ... power, yes, but also calm and relaxed around the gates, like an eddy within a waterfall....

#16: straight down, keep the bow up....

#17: upstream gate, unstable water, stay tight and wrap right around the pole....

At the end of the 1978 season, Jon intensified his preparation for the 1979 Worlds. In addition to doing plenty of paddling and lifting weights, he did two sets of exercises five times a week: 25 pullups, 30 situps, and 60 dips between chairs.

He also began an ambitious mental exercise, in which he studied past whitewater competitions. He memorized all the scores, not just for the C-1's, but for all the classes.

He explains: "I was looking for anything to work on, anything to make me better. Also, I was trying to see what the competition had done. I totally immersed myself in the sport, learning all the patterns so there wouldn't be any surprises. I also analyzed my strokes, not just the forward ones but all of them, trying in particular to find ways to get more extension on them."

In 1979, at Jonquiere, Quebec, after two years of intense Endicottism, American C-1's swept the medals (1,2,3 and 5). Establishing a pattern that would be oft-repeated in the next decade, two Brookmont kids—Jon Lugbill and Davey Hearn—finished one-two. "We responded to Bill's teachings," says Jon, "because we'd always known that our sport—unlike, say, flatwater paddling—allowed us to spend the day having a blast in the waves and still derive benefits for our racing."

Endicott's influence on Lugbill has been considerable. More than just improving his S-turn or teaching him how to maneuver properly through an upstream gate, he has totally reworked the way the paddler views himself. "The aim of self-image training," Endicott says, "is simply to help the athlete discover the 'real me,' and then to make his aspirations consistent with that realistic self image. The nervous system acts as a sort of computer, automatically setting out to accomplish whatever goal you program into it. If you program it with a negative image, it will produce negative results. Conversely, if you program it with a successful image, it will produce successful results. It's based on the principle that the subconscious mind cannot tell the difference between a real experience and one that is vividly imagined. Thus, by imagining things accurately ahead of time, the boater achieves the equivalent of many practice runs down the course."

"If some event in the future is causing stress for me," Lugbill says, "I visualize myself doing it very well. I visualize success, people patting me on the back. Once I can do something in my mind, I can do it for real."

Ironically, at the heart of this mind-riveting intensity, there is serenity. If Jon can truly relax—rather like locating the eye of the hurricane—his natural instincts will dominate and he will win. "Sometimes when you're mentally prepared, it feels like you're blah, like you're not too sharp. In reality, it's a signal that you've done the right things."

Bill Endicott believes that there are three crucial skills needed to excel in slalom paddling and that Jon Lugbill possesses all three. "First," he says, "you need great eye/paddle coordination—the ability to recognize water formations and be able to put the paddle exactly where you want, at the angle you want. Jon has tremendous eyes. I don't, so I appreciate the difference.

"Second, upper-body strength, particularly good shoulder and torso strength and good hip flexors. When you're ducking and dodging gates, it's important to be able to move the hips quickly. Jon is the perfect size for a slalom canoeist, not too big to slow the boat, yet with sufficient muscle to supply the explosive power needed for start-and-stop paddling. In flatwater paddling, the biggest guys have the advantage: but in whitewater—where it's power, power, and more power—a high strength-to-weight ratio is important.

"Third, Jon has an athletic mentality. He's psychologically laid back in the right places, doesn't get panicky. He can adjust quickly, which is very important in a sport where the course is moving all the time."

Lugbill has his own ideas on why he has excelled as a paddler. "First of all, it's always been fun for me," he says: "Oh, except when I was a little 11-year-old kid lugging a 35-pound boat around—that wasn't too much fun. But the boats got lighter and I got stronger, and now I don't even think about that."

Jon Lugbill is unusual in his ability to extract fun from the act of arising at 6:30 a.m. on a winter morning, trooping a mile down to a half-frozen Feeder Canal and going guts-out through the frigid spray until his heart beat maxes out and he's grimacing and snorting like a madman.

"It's all part of Jon's mystique," Endicott asserts, "his true grit. In winter you might see him out barefoot in old shorts."

Another quality that Lugbill believes separates him from the paddling masses is his ability to concentrate with every fiber of his being through 25 gates. "I never quit," he says, eyes dancing. "Never! I'm always pursuing that ultimate run. And always figuring it's the next one. The Europeans are catching up to us, to our training methods, so now more than ever I have to take chances and push the limits."

Endicott calls that extra Lugbill Push "Canoe Macho," a term Jon is clearly uncomfortable with. Without a paddle in his hands, the private Jon Lugbill is quite affable. He's kind to his English wife, Gill, and fond of his golden retriever, Jasper. All in all, he's the all-American Boy, the very antithesis of "macho." He would prefer to call the driving force that pulses within him simply "dedication." In elaboration, he says, "I'm just willing to work harder." That opinion becomes fact when one peruses the detailed records Endicott has kept of his team's progress. Prior to the 1979 Worlds in Jonquiere, for example, Lugbill averaged 42 practice sessions on the water per month. No other paddler was even close. Within each session he averaged 9.1 timed runs; all other paddlers averaged fewer than eight.

If that explains Lugbill's individual supremacy—grit, guts and determination—what of the group's supremacy? Why have the suburbs of Washington D.C. produced so many top-flight paddlers? How to begin to account for the 34 gold medals at the Worlds that the Brookmont kids have totaled since Endicott's arrivals? Coach has answered those questions so many times, the words roll smoothly off his tongue: "First, the Potomac itself. A good paddling river near a major metropolitan area. Rarely freezes, so it offers two paddling seasons for every one European season. Second, great parental support. The Lugbill parents used to go to all of Jon's races. Third, peer pressure. The area's gotten a reputation for great paddlers. Others come because they want to be part of that group dynamics. In other countries, paddlers train alone. Here it's strive together, thrive together. A sort of cooperative competition."

The main characters in that tableau are Davey Hearn and Jon Lugbill. The two dominant whitewater paddlers of the last decade are friendly but not close. They don't share racing secrets over pizza and beer, but then again they don't have to. They are already finely tuned to each other's strategy. Occasionally they'll discuss a technical point—like, say, "the angle of the paddle when feathering an entry duffek stroke"—and when they do, it's suggestive of a couple of nuclear physicists locked in a fission/fusion debate.

They are probably as convivial as two such intense rivals could possibly be. Their fierce competition, alone as they are in the exosphere of their sport, long ago canceled any chance of their becoming blood brothers. But they have shared so much—love of sport, success, neighborhood—that a mutual respect emerges from that. Says Lugbill: "Davey Hearn and I didn't get along too well in the beginning. I was a little more radical, go for it no matter what. He was more cautious, conservative. We've both moved toward the middle. Davey and I have the same desires, we think along the same lines."

"Sometimes I just wish he would go away," Hearn has said of Lugbill, "but that's not only a selfish attitude, it's a stupid one. If he weren't around, my training would be a lot harder."

Endicott enjoys telling of a particular Feeder Canal training session for which Lugbill was tardy. Archrival Davey Hearn was paddling well, but unspectacularly, and his times seemed to have leveled off. But when Lugbill arrived, Hearn proceeded to lower his personal record more than two seconds on a 70-second course.

ISERE RIVER: Gate #23: . . . A tricky downstream gate—watch the hole! . . . then a "bow draw" (which forces the top right hand over the outside left shoulder, placing the rotator cuff at risk) turns the boat sharp right . . . lift the bow up and slap down on the wave, then sprint to the next gate. . . .

Most of the original River Rats have retired or moved away now—except Davey Hearn and Jon Lugbill. Says Lugbill: "Of the original gang, only Davey and I have stayed here and stayed on top of it. We've remained innovative. Of course, it's easier to be innovative when you're ahead. When you're behind, it's psychologically harder to do something new."

It's not just doing something new, it's doing it better. Since 1979 Lugbill and Hearn have had a firm, exclusive grip on the gold and silver medals at the Worlds.

Despite a dual superiority that is unsurpassed in contemporary sports competition, the names Hearn and Lugbill are unknown except to the canoeing cogniscenti. With one exception, publicity has been limited to the "Faces in the Crowd" section at the back of Sports Illustrated or occasional articles in magazines like Canoe or Outside. That one exception is Lugbill's Wheaties box.

A few years ago, Wheaties, seeking new faces for its cereal boxes, began a "Search for Champions." The American Canoe Association, hoping for justice—and the $5,000 finder's fee—submitted Jon Lugbill's name. Says Lugbill of the experience: "Boxtops and letters from A.C.A. members all over the country got me into the top 50. Then Wheaties picked the final six, based on performance and character. I made it."

Whereas Mary Lou Rhetton received a six-figure payment for her appearance on Wheaties, Lugbill got a hearty handshake and a $400 plane ticket to Los Angeles: "The weird thing," he says with a cheerful shrug, "is that I was excited about it. I wanted to go train in the southern Sierra anyway."

Lugbill's cereal days lasted one month and 2 million boxes. "I like '2 million' better," he says, chuckling. "You say 'one month' and it doesn't sound like anything."

The dearth of accolades doesn't bother Lugbill—much. It did irritate him, however, that his "home" newspaper—the Washington Post—made no mention of his recent World Championship. Mostly, though, he just wants people to get the facts right. He has to live with the inevitably uninformed questions, like "Are you still whitewater rafting?" "Oh, well," he says, his natural acceptance of reality reemerging, "Why should they know the difference?"

No fame, no fortune. Why then does he do it? Lugbill gives the impression that he seldom asks himself that question. It's more of an instinctive thing—he works hard, sacrifices, suffers some, simply because he loves it. "I remember during the last Olympics skier Phil Mahre saying, 'I hate doing this. I only do it for the money. I'll never do it again.' Blah, blah, blah. I hate hearing that stuff. If you hate doing something don't do it. I don't care if you are making money, don't do anything you hate to do."

ISERE RIVER: ... #24, upstream gate, river left, poles hanging halfway over an eddy, part calm and part not ... drive real hard across it, then a stern-pivot turn to change directions quickly. ...

Last year in the U.S. about a dozen people died while whitewater canoeing. According to Endicott, almost every one of them was paddling in a group. "In some cases," he says, "there was even a doctor present. But if someone makes a mistake in the rapids, it can happen fast."

Lugbill admits that as a paddler he has all but transcended risk: "For me, whitewater rivers are very safe. I know how to put the boat, the paddle in just the right place. I personally have never come close to death in a boat. Never. For me to run Great Falls (on the Potomac) is very safe. But a beginner—someone without control of his stress level, who doesn't know the water—could die very easily at Great Falls. It's like a rabbit out on the highway that gets killed because it doesn't understand that the cars won't stop. It's the same for the average person going out on the river."

Lugbill, who has paddled over a 25-foot waterfall ("about as high as you can do without worrying about the impact"), says that the best way to stay alive on the river is the same as it's always been: "Before you get yourself into hard whitewater, make sure you have a bomb-proof roll."

Lugbill has visualized himself winning four C-1 World Championships and made it happen. Presently, he sees himself winning the 1989 Worlds, which, for the first time ever, will be held in U.S. waters (in Lugbill's own back yard, in fact, on Maryland's Savage River).

"I want to win in '89, so I'm going to keep training every day," he says. "If I take too much time off, I'll lose timing, power, technique. I used to paddle every single day for ten months. Now if I get sick, I'll take a day off—but only one."

It appears likely that whitewater slalom will reemerge in the 1992 Olympics in Spain. Will Jon Lugbill, who will only be 31, represent his country? "I don't know," he says: "It depends on whether I still like it. I know it's not going to be like it was when I was

14, it never is. On the other hand, why should I switch to another sport I'm not as good at? I wouldn't get that great Feeling."

ISERE RIVER: ... Gate #25, a forward gate ... lean back to get the bow up, keep it from burying ... overshoot gate and then come back into the current ... ahhh....

... Then the final agonizing crunch, a mighty sprint to the finish, ten seconds of anerobic hell, his heartbeat approaching 200, his muscles threatening mutiny....

Through the veil of pain, he hears the crowd yelling something ... what? ... they're yelling that he's already won the race, that his first run was good enough. "Good enough?" A self-canceling phrase. It could never be good enough.

Reaching deeper than ever before, Jon Lugbill's mind bullies his body to finish his second run in 200 seconds flat, bettering his closest competitor, Davey Hearn, by five seconds. More importantly to Lugbill, he has bettered his first run by two seconds. He has run fast and clean in both runs. He has sought and found the paddler's Grail: Controlled Aggression.

Credit: Gordon Wiltsie

Hackett nearing the top of the world

From the collection of Peter Hackett

Hackett with a sherpa pal

Credit: Yamaha

Roberts in a rare moment of repose

Randy Mamola in hot pursuit of Roberts

Credit: Bill Eggimann

Roberts displays his famous knee dragging style

Credit: Yamaha

Bachar hanging out in Yosemite

From the collection of John Bachar

The vertical world of John Bachar

Credit: Hughes Photography

Anderson en route to finishing the Western State 100

Anderson finishes the Pikes Peak Marathon, 1980

The dirty job of racing across America

Birdwoman

A young Jan Case at the Birdman Rally

Credit: Tony Trickle

Jon Lugbill at home in whitewater

Credit: Tony Trickle

The all-American boy

McKinney on the summit of Mustagh Alta, 25,000 feet

From the collection of Steve McKinney

McKinney breaks the world record at Cervina

It takes more than a bathing cap to be a triathlete.

Dave Scott and Mike Pigg in tandem

From the collection of Dave Scott

Ironman

From the collection of Rick Sylvester

Sylvester in mid-tumble between El Capitan and Yosemite

From the collection of Rick Sylvester

Sylvester takes a break with Roger Moore on the set of "For Your Eyes Only"

IRONMAN

"Mere survival is an affliction. What is of interest is
life, and the direction of that life."

—Guy Fregault

Moments before the start of the 1984 Hawaiian Ironman
Triathlon, Dave Scott waded out into the Pacific Ocean, drawing
stares and murmurs of recognition. Standing knee-deep in the
warm, blue water off Kailua Pier, he adjusted his swimming
goggles and shook out his well-developed shoulder muscles. It
was 6:55 a.m., and although the sun had not yet crept over Mt
Hualalai, the day was already warm. In an hour, when Scott was
due to emerge from the 2.4-mile ocean swim, it would be hot and
humid.

He kneaded a tight hamstring muscle and thought, "The
weather favors me. I'd rather do a triathlon in the Sahara than the
Arctic anyday...." After a while, old doubts began to assail him:
"Was he strong enough today to win? Would he feel bad early and
embarrass himself? Why did he put himself through all this?"
Seeking ablution, he dived into the water and washed away his
fears.

Submerged to the neck, he looked around at the other
competitors—more than 1000 well-toned bodies, men in yellow
bathing caps, women in red—moving into the sea like so many
lemmings. What drove them? Most, he figured, got by with what
he called the "Rocky philosophy"—just try to go the distance.

How different it was for him; he raced to win, especially in the Ironman, where he had done just that in 3 of the last 4 years.

It all began one night in 1978 when some Navy boys were whooping it up in an Oahu bar. Which of Hawaii's punishing endurance events, they wondered, was the toughest—the 2.4-mile Waikiki rough-water swim? The 112-mile around-Oahu bicycle race? Or the 26.2-mile Honolulu marathon? One of the men, Commander John Collins, suggested they separate the men from the boys by combining them all in a continuous 3-sport event. "It won't answer the question of which is the toughest event," he said, "but it will sure tell us who's the toughest human."

Thus, the Hawaiian Ironman was born. Fifteen men competed in the premiere contest. The battle for first was between two graduates of Navy "tough guy" squads, who nearly killed themselves trying to beat each other. The twelve finishers received a tiny trophy made of nuts and bolts with a hole in the top . . . that is, in the head.

In 1979, 14 men and one woman competed in the second Ironman. Despite the 11–16-hour "gruelathon" that the competitors faced, most brought a rather lighthearted attitude to the starting line. One man competed in a superman outfit; another in cow horns. And a third had taught himself how to ride a bicycle just the day before. But Tom Warren, who had once won a beer bet by doing 400 situps in a sauna, was dead-serious. He finished first in a time of 11 hours and 15 minutes.

Sports Illustrated covered that '79 Ironman, and in 1980—the year Wide World of Sports began televising the event—108 competitors showed up. By '82 the field had grown to 850. The following year, the Ironman started turning away thousands of applicants.

One of those who had read the S.I. article was 26-year-old Dave Scott of Davis, California. He was particularly moved by the description of one of the competitors, a man so depleted at the end of the race that he was stumbling into parked cars and accusing his support crew of trying to poison him. Certain that he could do better, Scott immediately went out and bought a bicycle and began training for the 1980 Ironman.

"Ever since I heard about the Ironman, I thought I could do it", he says. "I've always been a workout freak. In high school, whatever the coach said was gospel. I looked at Warren's times—3:50 in the marathon, which translates to nine-minute miles—and thought, 'I can do that.' I can be an exercise machine if I want to, and for the 1980 Ironman I wanted to."

He developed a three-sport exercise regimen so rigorous that it became legendary within the inner world of triathletes. Every week he bicycled 400 miles, swam 30,000 yards and ran 60-70 miles. In his spare time he lifted weights. All in all, he devoted 7 to 8 hours a day, six days a week, to training. "I had this idea that if I trained more than anyone else, I was bound to succeed. If I found out that Scott Tinley or Mark Allen were working out 50 hours a week, I'd work out 51. The real challenge of endurance sports lies in mustering the discipline necessary to train enough to win."

He was, as he says, bound to succeed. In the 1980 Ironman he led from start to finish, beating his closest competitor by more than an hour and shattering Warren's Ironman record by nearly two. "I knew the record was soft," he says modestly. "No one had ever seriously trained for a triathlon before. I realize I'd been working out my whole life for that event. The Ironman allowed me to show my true colors ... to find my niche."

MILE 0: As the clock ticked toward zero, some of the competitors began a countdown, while others prayed or cheered. "Five ... four ... three ... two ... one ... " The cannon boomed, launching more than a thousand swimmers as though shot from it. Beating the water to a white froth, they suggested fingerlings fighting for survival at a fish hatchery. In the vanguard, where the population density was lower, Scott and the other seeded athletes swam in water that was still blue, and relatively calm. Hawaiian waters are noted for their waves, but this day it was all roll and no chop. Scott figured he'd be out of the water in less than 52 minutes.

He slipped into third place in the lead pack of four. He was content there, bulling his way through the water with a powerful, steady 84 strokes per minute. He made by far the biggest splash, slapping the water each time as if the ocean were his enemy. It was Dave Scott's way of "beating the course."

He was fourth out of the water, but his transition (a fresh-water rinse, slip on socks and cycling cleats, eat a banana, pocket some figs) took less than two minutes and he was the second one out on his bicycle.

At the early stages of the ride, his "sea" legs were sluggish and unresponsive. Also the muscles of his upper body—the deltoids, the lats, the triceps—were pumped up, and he knew it would be several miles before they would relax. As he pedaled out onto the paved lava flats, one minute behind Mark Allen, he glanced at the second wave of athletes scurrying awkwardly toward their bikes, bananas in their mouths. Head down, he burrowed into a headwind.

Dave Scott lives in a cozy but cramped apartment in Davis with his new wife, Anna. The clues to his avocation are everywhere: the front porch is littered with running shoes and bicycle gear; the coffee table features magazines of his sports—*Runners World, Triathlon, Ultrasport*; the medicine cabinet is crammed with untold vitamins and minerals and the refrigerator is filled with exotic health foods. The bookcase contains—amidst the physiology tomes and the suspense novels—a dozen highly-organized scrapbooks and videotapes cataloging Scott's athletic career. "My Mom did it," he says. "She's my biggest fan. Both my Mom and Dad come to most of my races." One senses that, in Dave Scott's relations with his parents, the direction of influence has reversed itself. His mother has recently taken up running; his father, presently the president of the U.S. Triathlon Federation, is an accomplished cyclist, one of the best in the country in his age group.

Scott's parents, recognizing athletic prowess in their only son, encouraged—but never coerced—him. He started swimming when he was 7 and continued in age-group competition until he was 17. "I've spent a lot of time in the pool," says Scott. "But I never really felt that swimming was my forte. I've always had a horrendous stroke." At the University of California at Davis, he discovered another way to be competitive in the pool—water polo. He excelled to a point that in his junior and senior years he was named to the All-American team.

Meanwhile, as a physical-education major, he was learning a lot about physiology and kinesiology, useful knowledge for a triathlete. "I think my education gave me an enormous advantage over others." he says. "It gave me insight into the science of training. Knowing what muscles to emphasize, what foods to eat and supplements to take—it's enabled me to train more efficiently."

When you put in as many hours on the road as a triathlete does, minor orthopedic distractions can become full-blown injuries. "Triathlons magnify problem areas," says Scott. "You have to know how to train to avoid injuries. Runs should be first, swims last, because running pounds on your legs and if you do it after cycling you risk injury. But swimming—aahhh, it feels so good. Even when I feel fat and lazy, I can always swim."

Dave Scott lazy? Fat? At 6' and 163 (he balloons up to 165 in the winter as training time drops off), he appears to be all muscle, vein and sinew. He has the body of the classic male triathlete—with the thighs of a cyclist, the calves of a runner and the shoulders of a swimmer and lifter. The incongruous bulge around his middle—at first taken for a pot—is, in fact, an extra ridge of muscle. "I hate doing situps," Scott explains, "so I invented my own abdominal exercises. I do them in the pool."

MILE 20: Alone on the lava flats, five minutes behind Mark Allen, Scott pedaled smoothly, almost jauntily. He had a natural rhythm in cycling that he seemed to lack in swimming and running. Reaching into his pocket, he pulled out a fig and popped it into his mouth. Two squirts from the water bottle brought life back to his desiccated tongue. Suddenly the road dropped off, necessitating a gear change. Then another. He put his teeth to the bar and roared down the hill, imagining himself a torpedo slicing through the heavy air.

At the bottom of the hill, a right turn reared up. Scott leaned that way (threatening the "tire-adhesion breaking point"), then coasted through the turn without braking, his pedal an inch off the pavement. Righting himself, he shifted gears, then relaxed his grip on the handlebars and thought, "That was dangerous ... damn near planted a pedal ... yeah, dangerous ... and exciting."

People meeting Scott for the first time after viewing him on TV are invariably struck by his All-American good looks. At rest, his short blond hair is so tidy that he could be a model for "The Dry Look." He has a prominent nose, chiseled facial features and the healthy, bronze glow of a man who spends a lot of time outside. His expressive mouth, easy with a smile, reveals extraordinarily large white teeth.

When he hears—as he often does—that he's "much more handsome in person than on TV ," he smiles and says, "When I'm doing the Ironman—tongue hanging out, eyelids drooping, sweat dripping from every orifice—I just don't look my best."

Through clean living, proper training and a good deal of luck, Scott has managed to stay relatively free of injuries. But competing in, and training for, triathlons is inherently risky— particularly the cycling event. Once, while returning from a frigid cycling workout, Scott skidded on a pile of crushed olives and hit the pavement hard, gashing his left elbow and badly bruising his right hip. That kept him out for a month. Later, with the hip still healing, he was time-trialing, cycling smoothly at 25 mph, head down, eyes on the white line, when he hit a dead possum. He did a half-gainer over the handlebars, landing—once again—on the pavement and re-injuring his hip and elbow.

Another time, near the finish of a 200-kilometer bicycle race, Scott foolishly opted to bypass the last aid station—and became both dehydrated and hypoglycemic. Starting down a hill at 20 mph, his eyes blurred and he drifted off the winding road, crashing into a rock. He required 60 stitches in his head and a year to heal, but still refuses to wear a helmet unless the rules demand it. He explains: "I never train with one. It causes discomfort, which is the last thing I need out there."

Some would say that discomfort and the Ironman were synonymous. The race takes the average competitor more than 13 hours to complete, and the heat and humidity of Hawaii combine malevolently to sap the racer of precious bodily fluids. Every year about 10% of the starters become dropouts, and many more require medical care the moment they stumble, crawl or fall across the finish line.

Scott, who has never finished worse than second in the Ironman, has rarely experienced that kind of depletion. "My sweat glands work well," he admits. "And I process oxygen pretty efficiently...."

Though he is often accused of being a mental freak (as in, "anyone who pushes himself so hard must be wrong in the head"), the truth is that Scott is a physical freak. Along with only a few other top triathletes, bikers, rowers and cross-country skiers, he has a state-of-the-art respiratory system and a musculature dominated by slow-twitch—or endurance—fiber.

MILE 58: Scott, halfway through the bike race, was experiencing leg cramps. The wind had picked up and was gusting to 50 mph. No longer did he appear jaunty. His face had hardened into grim determination. What he was doing was just plain hard work. Ducking his head, driving his legs, he wondered just how far ahead Allen was. Nobody was around to tell him. Nobody was ever around. One thing about being a world-class triathlete, you had to get used to competing alone. Back in the pack, the sights and sounds of people filled the air; near the front with Dave Scott, there was only the metallic whirring of a bicycle sprocket, the roar of the wind, the beating of his heart. Scott dug deep within his well-developed imagination, focusing his mental pictures until he clearly saw himself gaining on Mark Allen.

When explaining his skills in the context of the nature-nurture dichotomy, Scott favors the latter. "I think my diet makes a big difference—it's about 75% carbohydrate, 10% fat and the rest protein. No sugar, oil, white flour or red meat." Scott's formidable daily exertion burns up more than 6,000 calories, yet he refuses to eat most high-caloric foods. He compensates with gluttonous quantities of fruits and vegetables. "I like fish, but I won't cook it myself. I eat chicken a couple of times a year. Mostly it's fruit and vegetable salads, tofu, rice crackers, yogurt and cottage cheese."

The Dave Scott legend includes lurid tales of his downing 17 bananas for an appetizer . . . 5 salads for dinner . . . and washing his cottage cheese. "Yes, I wash my cottage cheese," he says, with a shy laugh. "Rinsing reduces the fat by about 10% and eliminates some of the salts. I mean I don't hose it off in the front yard or anything; I put it in a strainer.

"I eat well, but I'm not a fanatic. I'll drink wine and beer when the time is right. I even go to parties once in a while, though I'm not the type to writhe around on the floor. . . . People ask me what I think about while I'm training—I tell them I think of my body rhythms . . . and lunch."

Before a "short" triathlon—anything less than three hours—Scott runs on empty. "I consume only water," he says. "For an Ironman, I'll eat heavily up to two days before. On the morning of the race, I'll have three bananas, toast, water. Then during the race, it's about 20 figs and a couple of bananas on the bike, a banana and some orange slices on the run . . . and lots of water! At least a couple of gallons, more if I can get it."

Viewers of the '83 Ironman saw an annoyed Dave Scott—22 miles into the run, 136 miles into the race—throw down the cup of Gatorade he'd been handed and call for water. "The electrolyte drinks are a lot of bull," he says. "They have too much sugar and too high a concentration of minerals. They can't be assimilated into the body quickly enough. They'll actually draw water from the muscles to the stomach, making you more dehydrated."

MILE 78: Scott, calves bulging, stood up in his stirrups and pedaled powerfully up the hill, trying to slice into Mark Allen's 10-minute lead. He felt strong, much better than in 1983. He'd lost 8 minutes to Allen on the bike, but he wasn't worried. The bike was Allen's best event, the run was Scott's, and best of all, only he knew it.

He and the bike were working as one now, a fluid, efficient machine, needing lubrication. He sucked on his water bottle and searched for an aid station.

Just then he spotted Allen, who was heading back from the turnaround at Hawi. Scott knew that this moment of passing was of key psychological importance. It was one of the few times in the race that competitors were able to see one another, to read one another. Allen had the lead, but he had to be hurting too. If he saw pain or weakness in the face of Scott, it could give him the boost he needed to win. As they passed, both men wore masks of benign indifference.

Winning the Ironman in '80, '82 and '83 brought Dave Scott fame, but no fortune; prestige, but no prize money. Until recently, the Hawaiian Ironman had never offered a purse, apparently on the theory that just having the opportunity to "go the distance" is reward enough. Although most triathlons do offer some prize money, purses are still quite small, and as yet no triathlete has been able to make a good living from his winnings.

Scott has found other ways. The quantitative leap in the popularity of triathlons brought out neophytes in droves, and soon budding triathletes were pestering him to design training programs for them. They phoned from all over the country, asking for his secrets; at first he gave them away, then he began charging—$200 to design a one-year regimen, $500 to run an all-day clinic.

After his first Ironman win, Scott attracted four sponsors, each of whom paid him "a little" money. Nike, Bell (helmets), Peak Performance (vitamins), and Anheuser-Busch each paid him about $1500. "Triathletes aren't yet identifiable to the masses," says Scott. "But our day will come. Right now, there are about 15–20 triathletes making a living off the sport. Make that a partial living. Sharing houses, driving old cars. . . ."

Triathletes would seem to have plenty of products to endorse. During a race, they are forever changing their outfits, and in the area of gadgets they use everything from swimming goggles to bicycle helmets. That is, most do. Dave Scott doesn't. While it's not uncommon to see the other top triathletes wearing wet suits on the swim, Scott wears only his trunks. On the bicycle, the latest craze is the sleek, aerodynamic tear-drop helmet, but Scott rides bare-headed whenever he can. Although it may hurt his advertising, he believes it helps him race.

Until recently, when legal troubles intervened, a handful of top triathletes were being subsidized by the sport's Sugar Daddy: JDavid, an investment securities company based in San Diego. JDavid had under contract five of the top six male triathletes and two of the top five women. The members of Team JDavid were treated with the veneration of potential Olympians. They trained and traveled together; they received equipment, free clothes and all-expenses-paid trips to Nice and Hawaii for competitions, as well as a stipend of about $1200 a month. They typically arrived in Hawaii 10 days before the Ironman, with an entourage that included a cook and a team bike mechanic.

The comforts and advantages afforded Team JDavid make Dave Scott's accomplishments all the more remarkable, for he was the lone top male Triathlete absent from the team. Yet in 1982 he won all 10 of his races, including his second Ironman, training alone. . . .

On a cold, wet, windy morning, a lone runner jogs down a narrow country road. A tule fog hangs low over the rice fields, creating a monochromatic moonscape. The only splashes of color are the runner's green vest and blue gloves, antidotes for the damp cold that seeps into his bones. Head down, he plows ahead on his 8th mile of the day, his 62nd of the week.

He's tired—dull from fatigue—and glad it's Saturday. Sixty miles to go on the bike . . . a two-mile swim . . . then he'll take Sunday off. Spend some time with Anna, maybe watch a football game. Be an ordinary person for a day.

His run turns to a plod. He is still two miles from his apartment, but now he's just putting one foot in front of the other, trying to go the distance. His thoughts are uncharacteristically negative: "Why is it always windy in Davis? ... Maybe I'm training too much...."

Suddenly, ahead in the distance, he spots another runner—a ghost shrouded in mist. He squints to make sure, then confirming that he and the figure are moving in the same direction, he begins to sprint, to close the gap. The race is on and he is born anew.

Scott says it would be a mistake to label him a recluse. "Contrary to what is written about me, I do miss the human contact of training with others. It's lonely out there on the windswept roads of rural Davis; but there are competitive advantages to the solitude and the bad weather. The members of Team JDavid knew about each other's strengths and weaknesses, but they didn't know about mine. Working out alone, I've been able to maintain a certain mystique. For example, there was a time when running was my weakest event. But I worked on it and got better and even had some races in which I caught Tinley, Allen or Molina on the run. Sure, those guys trained under perfect conditions in San Diego, but when they got to the Kona Coast for the Ironman, it must have seemed like the moon. I was already used to the moon."

MILE 92: Approaching one of the 28 aid stations, Scott signalled to the volunteers, and when he pedaled by, they were dutifully lined up, reaching toward him with cups of water and wet sponges. Slowing only slightly, he deftly snatched the prizes from their hands. While he cooled himself with the water from a sponge, he drank two cups of water. He knew about dehydration.

Dave Scott—handsome, humble, articulate—is the perfect triathalon ambassador. In numerous interviews and articles, his infectious enthusiasm for the sport spills forth. He once said, "I encourage all of you Ironmen—and other triathletes—to strive for your goals, whether they be to win or just to try ... The trying is everything."

During Scott's reign as "Ironman," the sport has evolved from an activity perceived as suitable only for the type of people who howl at the moon or laugh in all the wrong places to one in which millions of people in at least thirty countries now participate. In 1982, in the U.S. alone, 60,000 people participated in 250 triathlons. A year later, the numbers were four times that. In 1986, 1.2 million Americans are expected to take part in 2,100 triathlons, making it the fastest growing participatory sport in America. "It's exploding," Scott says. "In a few years it will be as big as tennis."

Scott envisions the day when world-class triathletes will command the six-figure appearance money that, say, Joan Benoit gets for running the Chicago Marathon. "It'll happen," he says. "The sport is still in its infancy. Running has taken years to advance to the point of high recognition. One of the problems with triathlons has been that there are no standardized lengths or world records for people to identify with. The transitions are all different, the water temperatures are all different...."

The athletes, too, are different. Research indicates that triathletes have slower metabolic rates, stronger hearts, denser bones and more money than the average person. According to *Triathlon* magazine, the average triathlete makes $45,000 a year, has graduated from college and carries an American Express card. Over a third of the entrants in the Ironman are attorneys, airline pilots, doctors, dentists, engineers, business owners, educators and stockbrokers. As one race organizer explained, "It's a natural extension of the aggression these people take to their careers."

But when you're Dave Scott, professional triathlete, it is a career. And getting up at 6:30 on a frozen foggy morning to bicycle 80 solitary miles is part of it. Like all workers, Scott sometimes feels like calling in sick. "I'm human," he insists. "Some days I just feel like sitting in my beanbag chair and letting the day go by."

In spite of his protests, Scott lets few days go by. He is used to digging deep within for his sources of strength. Moreover, he believes that if you're in shape, an Ironman is not just 140 miles of pain and mental anguish. If you're in shape, his theory goes, there are morphine-like highs to be reaped. A sense of power. A feeling that one can go on forever.

But what if you're not in shape? The other side of the coin must be some kick-ass lows. "The 1983 Ironman," Scott says, nodding his head. "My hardest race. No one believes it, but I was in lousy shape. In the previous six months I had missed more days than I had trained. And the winds that day were the worst. I won the race, but when I got to the finish I had absolutely nothing left. Everything was a blur. I tried to wave to some friends and nearly tipped over. I beat Tinley by 33 seconds (in the closest Ironman ever), but if the race had been a hundred yards further it would have been his. They carried me to the medical tent and pumped me full of glucose. I was in bad shape."

MILE 112: With a little more than two miles to go on the bike, Scott lowered his head into a 50-mph gust of wind. Focusing on the white line, he cautioned himself: "Be patient . . . Allen is great on the bike . . . don't burn out with a final sprint . . . there's still a marathon to go . . . pace!"

He knew to win he'd have to be the consummate tactician. Ease up too much on the bike and you need five-minute miles on the run . . . ride too hard and you die on the run . . . don't drink enough and you don't even get to the run. . . .

"I always have a race plan when I begin," he has said, "but with so many variables, that race plan usually gets tossed early. Your goggles get knocked off . . . someone crosses in front of you . . . a flat tire. It's very important for a triathlete to be able to adapt. Other competitors let those unanticipated events wear them down. I can see it taxing them, and I guess I delight in being a part of that wearing-down process. I'll think to myself: I feel as bad as they do, but I know I can go a little further . . . then a little further. It's not pain if you're in shape—it's only high-level discomfort.

"I think Allen is my most formidable opponent, the most mentally tough, but even he doesn't scare me. I do. Myself. I can talk myself out of training, working hard. My primary motivator is to live up to my own standards. I create the fear that lives within me."

When Scott began doing triathlons, his best sport was swimming, his worst cycling. In response to that, he worked hard on the bike, and after a while cycling was his strongest event. But this made his running look shabby, so he went to work on it. "I think it's interesting that I'm basically mediocre in three events, yet when you put them together I can be the best in the world. I tend to work close to my limits at all times. . . .

"Well, maybe not mediocre, but hardly world-class. My best time in the marathon is 2:33. If I worked at it, I could probably get down to 2:25—but that isn't even 'United States-class.' "

MILE 114.4: Scott rolled into the bike-run transition area in 5 hours and 10 minutes. Before he had come to a stop, he had already kicked off his cycling shoes, and his sweat-soaked jersey was up around his neck. He was 11 minutes behind Mark Allen, solidly in control of second place. His mask of grim determination suggested he was dissatisfied but not discouraged. As he hustled inside to towel down and speed-tie the laces of his running shoes, TV commentators outside reminded the public that running was Dave Scott's worst event. Scott knew better.

Starting the run, his legs were rubbery, defiant. He was well aware that the most difficult transition was from bike to run. For 5 hours, his leg muscles had been repeating a specific motion; for 112 road miles, the bike had supported his weight—but now his legs had to do that. Leaving the hotel parking lot, the road immediately began to climb. Dave Scott followed, searching for an easy running rhythm. He knew it would be several miles before he found it.

Despite JDavid's attempts to instill camaraderie into the sport, world-class triathletes remain highly individualistic. Like most triathletes, Scott was drawn to a sport that forces the athlete to work things out for himself. "In a triathlon, it's all up to the competitor," he points out. "The longer the race, the greater the challenge. I think I have the mental perseverance to out-endure anybody in the Ironman. For most, the topography at Kona is mentally stifling and they lose their concentration after about five hours. They give up."

MILE 120: The heat shimmers off the pavement, creating mirages in the distance; the only sound in the hot heavy air is the steady squish-squish-squish of Scott's shoes as they hit the pavement. Nearly six miles into the run, he is striding smoothly—as smoothly as he is able. For under the best of conditions, his technique in the run, like the swim, is heavy, brutish. The way he pounds the pavement and swings his head from side to side is not textbook stuff. He is, in fact, a classic example of strength and endurance taking precedence over form.

Although Scott is 33, newly married and writing a book, he doesn't talk retirement. First of all," he predicts, "my age won't be a factor for a long time. The peak for triathletes is going to be older than for most other sports. It takes years to become proficient, plus there's no real physiological reason to collapse. Motivation is the biggest thing, but I still have that. I'll do 10 or 11 races this year. My goal now is to be dominant at all distances. Not just the long, endurace races, where only 'empty-headed Dave Scott' can do well. I want to win every triathlon that I enter this year."

While most triathletes worry only about completing the race, Scott regards that as a given. He has finished 98 of the 100 triathlons he has started. Explaining his remarkable inner drive, he says, "I get a self-satisfaction in pushing myself to the near-limits of my capabilities. When I do that, I find I can be among the best in the world. I have an ego like everyone else."

MILE 130: The ABC people, cruising around in their flatbed trucks, told Scott that Allen's lead had shrunk to six minutes, that he was complaining of leg cramps, that at times he was slowing to a walk. The news gave Scott a remarkable jolt. He could feel it entering his body, like some wonder drug, like some magical combination of cortisone and adrenaline, working its way through his heart, lungs, legs and mind. Like a cheeta stalking his prey, he picked up the pace and set out after Allen.

ULTRA-MARATHONER

"One of the misfortunes of advancing age is
that you get out of touch with the sunrises ... "
—John Buchan

SQUAW VALLEY, CALIFORNIA, JUNE 28, 1986, 4:45 A.M.:
Milling about on the edge of the pack of 400-plus runners is Ruth
Anderson, a tall, lean, older woman with boyishly-cut platinum
hair and a dazzling smile. At 56 she is the oldest female entrant, but
she is also a bouncy, vibrant woman who appears ten years
younger than her age. She is back for her fourth try at the Western
States 100-Miler, a run many call "the toughest endurance event in
the world."

Anderson wears Nike running shoes, red shorts, a windbreaker and a "fanny pack," (filled with four pint bottles of water,
granola bars, M & M's, peanuts, ankle tape, Vaseline, and Chap-
stick). Unlike most of the other runners, she does no stretches, as if
she prefers to save herself for the run itself; instead she greets old
friends, laughing and chatting about past runs. Considering the
physical and psychological ordeal she faces, she appears extraordinarily centered—excited but not uptight, intense but not
demonic. She has, of course, been here before and that helps.

In a race in which the real measure of success is whether or not
one has the stuff to finish before the official 30-hour cutoff, Anderson is only one for three. But no other woman her age is even in the
running.

The classic late bloomer, she never even ran around the block until she was 43 years old. As a young girl in Nebraska, she played field hockey and was a state-ranked junior tennis player. But one of the first things she learned after coming west to enroll at Stanford was to forget about a tennis career—in California she was just another player.

She studied math and science, ultimately taking the job she now holds as a radiochemist at the Lawrence Livermore Radiation Lab, southeast of San Francisco. Her work consists of analyzing the gamma radiation given off by various substances—everything from environmental impact micro-analysis to the evaluation of underground nuclear explosions. She finds the work interesting, but clearly would rather talk about running.

"I've always had an appreciation for sports," she says, "but for twenty years I limited my participation to light tennis and swimming. Then in 1972, they closed the Lab pool for the winter and two lady co-workers urged me to run with them during lunch hour.

"I'll never forget that first run—eight minutes for a little more than a mile. I've never smoked, but I coughed all afternoon, like I'd never really breathed before. I thought I was dying. I said to myself: 'They'll never get me out there again.' But two days later I was at it again, and in two weeks they had me up to two miles. Two months after that, I entered a novice two-mile race and made it in 15½ minutes. I was hooked."

Those noon runs along the country roads of Livermore soon became a fixture in Anderson's life. After six months she had increased her distance to 40 miles a week. When she ran 20 miles in 2½ hours, she became convinced that she could run a marathon in less than 3:30. Then she found out that the world's record for over-40 women was 3:29:07, and that became her goal. Two months later, she entered her second marathon, the 1973 Fiesta Bowl in Phoenix, Arizona.

Flashing perfect white teeth and pale blue eyes, her face radiates the excitement she felt during that race: "At 10 miles I was four minutes under a 3:30 pace . . . at 20 miles, seven minutes under . . . I knew then that I could do it. The realization was thrilling."

She finished in 3:26:07, a new world's record for women over 40. Three years later, she lowered that mark to 3:10:10. And in 1978, at the age of 49, she ran a 3:04 marathon—a 7-minute mile pace. In all, she has run 75 marathons. "I don't know whether I'll reach 100 or not," she says with uncharacteristic doubt. "For me the marathon is the most difficult distance—it requires speed as well as endurance. And I have to face it: I just don't have great leg speed."

Ever since 490 B.C., when Pheidippides ran 26 miles, delivered the message of a military victory at Marathon, then fell dead, the marathon has been regarded as the ultimate test of endurance. But Ruth has run further than that—ultra-marathons—30 times. In 1975 she ran a 50-kilometer race in 4 hours, 17 minutes. In 1978 she ran 100 miles on a track in a world age-group record 16:50:47. She was the first woman accepted in the London to Brighton 54-Miler, finishing it in 7:46:16; and in 1980, she ran in the National 50-Mile Championships in Houston, cutting 15 minutes off her best time and setting another world record for 50-year-old women.

But all of that was merely a warmup for the ultimate Ultra, the Western States Endurance Run, 100 arduous trail miles from Squaw Valley to Auburn, through snow drifts and rivers, a punishing combination of 17,040 feet of uphill and 21,970 feet of downhill.

SQUAW VALLEY, 4:59 A.M.: At the start of the Western States you can't help noticing the lighting. On the eastern horizon, there is a faint pre-dawn glow, a subtle mix of pinks and blues; but as you near the starting line, that is overpowered by camera flashes and the abrasive glare of ABC's floodlights. Adding to this eerie effect, almost all the runners carry flashlights.

Next, you are struck by how old the runners are. Some appear to be past their salad days. The race program reports that seven of the male entrants are in their sixties and that the average Western States runner is more than 36 years old. In 1985 three of the top ten finishers were in their forties, and one, Doug Latimer, was 48.

War whoops greet the gun which sounds the start of the race. At the head of the pack, movement is swift and sure—the best runners will finish in 16–18 hours—but back in the middle of the pack with Ruth, movement is fitful—walk, run, stop—suggestive of a post-game crowd leaving a packed stadium.

After a time, however, the crowd disperses and Anderson finds her niche, widening her stride and settling into a pace best described as "a brisk walk." She is content with that for now, as the first 4.7

miles of the course is a steep 3,700-foot climb to Emigrant Gap, and she worries about burning out too early.

Although the temperature in Auburn that day will reach 90 degrees (and 100 in the canyons of the run), it is—at 5:30 a.m.—cool and breezy. Many runners, thinking only of the afternoon heat, are shivering in shorts and a singlet or T-shirt. Ruth, increasing her pace to a trot, zips up her windbreaker, thankful that she remembered to bring it.

The Western States Endurance Run is only 13 years old, but for the past 30 years the trail has been the course for the Western States 100-Mile Ride (the Tevis Cup), a world-famous horse race. It was started by Wendell Robie, a lumberman, banker, and outdoorsman. In 1973 Robie received a call from the head of the Marine Corps training unit at Fort Wayne requesting permission to have 20 of his top Marine trainees try to cover the 100-mile distance in 48 hours, commencing the day before the Tevis Ride.

Of the 20 Marines who started, only two finished.

Sitting in the audience at the Tevis banquet when the Marines stood up and received applause from the riders was Gordy Ainsleigh, a 22-year-old woodcutter, who had ridden in the Tevis Cup twice, running with his horse as much as riding it. Ainsleigh was convinced that he could best the Marines, so the following year he left his horse at home and ran the Tevis Cup on foot. He completed the distance in 23 hours, 42 minutes, beating many of the horses to the finish line.

By 1977, word of Ainsleigh's feat had spread through the ultra-distance running community. Fourteen runners applied to run the Tevis Cup, which marked the official beginning of the Western States Endurance Run.

Only three finished.

Since then, participation and interest in the Western States has increased dramatically. The 1986 field of 400-plus included men and women from 41 states and four foreign countries. Despite the stringent requirements (entrants must pass a physical exam and have run a 50-mile race in less than 10 hours), more than 800 men and women have applied to run the past few years. The field is reduced by lottery, though race management reserves the right to "admit participants who have contributed significantly to the event, or whose participation will significantly enhance the competition"—say, for example,

Ruth Anderson.

In 1980 two male friends in their sixties talked Anderson into running the Western States with them, then dropped out a week before the race with injuries, leaving her to run it without the support of friends. About fifty miles into the course, she slipped in the heavy snow and fell against a pine tree, wrenching her back and temporarily ending her quest.

She returned the next year: on the day of the race, the temperature in Auburn soared to 101. There was a shortage of water, air, everything but heat. Ruth had trouble keeping fluids down and at the 60-mile mark began vomiting. When the medics weighed her, they discovered she'd lost more than the permitted seven percent of her 124 pounds. She was declared dehydrated and yanked from the race.

The evening before the 1983 Western States-100, after Ruth had been signed in, weighed and briefed, she and her daughter decided to walk the first couple of miles of the course. It was almost dusk and no one else was around. Suddenly an explosion ripped through the stillness of the forest. "It sounded like an avalanche," Ruth remembers. "A gigantic rotten log had broken loose and was rolling down the mountain right at us! ... terrified, we started running downhill ... the log hit a tree and broke in two, which gave it backspin ... when it finally came to a stop it was about ten feet away from us! ... " Anderson was so shaken, she almost didn't run the next day, but then her unbounded optimism kicked in: "I thought, 'Hey, it didn't get me, so it must be a good omen.'"

Next morning before the race, she effusively told anyone who'd listen, "Just as you guys are about to turn the first mile there at the bridge, take a look at that gigantic log. It was intended for me, but it didn't get me!"

That year she confronted the worst conditions yet: 25 miles of trail were still covered with snow. "I fell down about a million times," she remembers, "but I paced myself, held the nausea to a minimum and made it in less than 30 hours to earn my plaque."

In addition to winning a plaque for finishing the race in less than thirty hours, a Western-States runner can win a silver belt buckle by finishing in less than twenty-four hours. Ruth has long coveted that silver belt buckle. "It certainly is the running goal that looms largest for me," she admits, still smiling. "Sure, I'm proud of a plaque for finishing that rascal, but, darn it, I really want to get under twenty-four hours and win that silver belt buckle!"

MILE 30, 12:10 P.M.: Ruth Anderson lopes into Robinson Flat, six minutes under a 24-hour pace and feeling fine. The first major checkpoint of the run, it suggests a war camp: panting, perspiring, even wounded people litter the area in partial states of undress, taking nourishment and receiving medical aid. About 20 runners have already dropped out, and one man who took a bad fall has had to be helicoptered out with a broken rib and a punctured lung.

The doctors are required to weigh Ruth; she is ushered to the medical area, where she removes her fanny pack and steps on the scale. "One-twenty-two. Minus two pounds." She is pleased, for had she lost too much weight, they'd have wanted to take her pulse and blood pressure too, and there was no time to waste on that stuff....

Just then Ruth's voluntary support crew—two friends from San Diego—rush up to her, full of solicitous inquiries. She tells them that she is fine, feeling pretty strong, but that her feet are wet and that she has a slight muscle spasm in her right calf from fording frigid streams. As arranged, the friends have one of the six drop bags that Anderson has had packed into various checkpoints. While she sits and has a deviled-egg sandwich and some coffee, they change her shoes and socks for her. The sun by now is high in the cloudless sky, and Anderson hastily removes her long-sleeved shirt and puts on a singlet and scarf. After another moment of deep breathing, she straps on her fanny pack and waves good-bye to her friends, regaining the trail to Deep Canyon and immediately looking forward to her daughter Rachel's aid station at Dusty Corners. Time of pit stop: 11 minutes.

Ruth has long been one of the moving forces in the effort to secure equal rights for women runners—especially Masters (over 40) women runners. Although she denies that she is a political person, her commitment to The Movement is obvious. "The excitement of being part of the emergence of Masters women in long-distance running," she effuses, "was like being an explorer landing in fascinating new territory. When I began in the sport, there was age-group competition for men, but not for women. Men over 40 had been enjoying ten-year and even five-year divisions in major races for years, but what about women? We don't stay 39 forever. For so long I heard the argument that there weren't enough over-40 women to merit separate divisions ... well, we showed that to be false.

"I was motivated by the obvious injustices in women's running that needed correcting—particularly in Masters. The pervasive attitude among the AAU committee members was that women were fragile things that shouldn't be allowed to run distances longer than a mile. Nonsense! Women have been running marathons for years. How can you tell a woman who's been doing something for years that she's too fragile to be 'recognized' for doing it?"

Ruth continued to hammer at AAU members, arguing that they needed a women's long-distance chairman at the national level. Partly through her efforts, the First Women's National AAU Marathon Championship was held in 1974. In 1975, the AAU recognized "Masters women" as a championship category. That same year, Ruth attended the first brainstorming session for the purpose of putting a women's marathon into the Olympics. The movement finally succeeded in 1984.

Ruth herself has broken the sex barrier in several races, most notably the highly traditional London-to-Brighton 54-Miler. "I had long dreamed of doing that double-marathon," she says, "but in the 29-year history of that race they had never permitted a woman to run. I resolved to change that. Being my usual persistant self, I kept writing letters to the British Road Runners Club, who sponsors the event. I finally convinced them to open it up."

In 1980, Ruth and four other women joined 136 men in that race. Afterward, the reporters gathered around Ruth, who, with her usual bubbly charm, regaled them with stories. When asked if she were glad that the race was over, she told them, "Something anticipated with such ardor is always over too soon."

MILE 56, 7:20 P.M.: Stumbling into the Michigan Bluff checkpoint area, Ruth is 55 minutes over a 24-hour pace and feeling terrible. She is sick to her stomach, a symptom that has often assailed her on long runs. She forces down a cup of her special tea concoction, but it tastes so sweet that it makes her gag. She drinks some water, but that makes her throw up. The medics persuade her to try something she ordinarily shuns—a carbonated soft drink. After awhile she begins to feel

better, though still as weak as a baby bird. Supine and limp beneath a
tree, she watches as other runners pass by, giving her the same wan
smiles she was giving others just two hours earlier. Yes, she thinks,
matters can deteriorate quickly out here. I was feeling so good only a
few miles ago—what went wrong? Somehow fatigue in the lower
back seems to lead to nausea, which leads to collapse. . . .

Sitting up, she forces back pain and fatigue. She thinks, "Just
get up and keep moving. You've been here before. The worst thing is
to sit and feel sorry for yourself . . . " She drags herself to her feet and
straps on her fanny pack. Slowly, stiffly, she moves down the trail.
Time of pit stop: 17 minutes.

While non-participants marvel at the discipline needed to complete a
race like the Western States, Ruth seems to take it for granted. "It's
come to me naturally," she says. "You don't go into math and science
without discipline. . . . No, I never had to go to classes on motivation.
In fact, I recently spoke on this topic at a psychology class. I was on
the ticket with a member of the Harlem Globetrotters, who claimed
he was motivated by economics. I told them that wasn't even an issue
in ultramarathoning."

Though Ruth earns no money from her sport, she has an entire
room in her Oakland home devoted to the trophies, plaques and
ribbons that she has won over the years. Rewarding, yes, but clearly it
takes more than prizes to induce someone to run a race as grueling as
the Western States.

Laughing her easy, childlike laugh, she agrees, "It helps to
receive a plaque or a trophy, to get some recognition, but in the
Western States the motive is confronting the challenge. Running has
been a way for me to test myself. The initial challenge for me was just
to be able to run two miles, then six, then 20 . . . then a marathon in
less than 3:30. Goals are the perfect motivator."

For many people, the barrier to long-distance running is, in a
word, boredom. Ruth, however, says she rarely gets bored, even on
the longest runs. "Certainly in trail running, I've never known
boredom. It's simply too beautiful. I've always been a natural fantas-
izer, and when I get out there among the flowers, I have lovely
fantasies.

"Running the track isn't beautiful, but it's very social and I love
it. You have your support crew every quarter-mile . . . friends . . .

music, it's great . . . still, twenty-four hours on the track is my limit. I prefer the flowers."

Ruth Anderson is unusual in her ability and willingness to run both track and trail. In 1982, she captained and ran for a 10-woman team in a Masters Women's 24-hour race, which set a world record of 202.87 miles. (The last two hours of the race were run in driving wind and rain as the tail of Hurricane Eva hit the Sacramento area.) Her first solo 24-hour run was a charity affair at the Santa Rosa Junior College track in which she completed 110 ¼ miles. In addition, she belongs to the World Association of Veteran (Masters) Athletes, which every other year since 1975 has held a world championship in track-and-field and cross-country. In Rome, in 1985, Ruth ran distances from 1500 meters to a marathon.

"Next year the competition will be in Melbourne, Australia," Anderson says, her eyes brightening at the prospect. "I may go as low as 800 meters again, but there are specialists who can eat me up. My best time in the mile is less than six minutes, but I'm best in the longer distances. I've signed up for six events . . . just in case."

Some researchers believe women have the potential to achieve parity with men at the longer distances. One authority, Dr Ernest van Aaken, a German physician, biochemist and prolific sports medicine writer, says the greatest female advantage in distance running will appear in the 50-to-100 mile range. Dr Joan Ullyot, an American cardiovascular research physician and runner, agrees: "After the body burns carbohydrates and protein, it is left with fat—the reserve tank. Women carry more fat than men and burn it slower, so that at the 20-mile mark when men seem to run out of gas, women don't. If you take a man and a woman who have the same time in a 10-mile race and put them in a marathon, the woman will usually win."

MILE 78, 1:00 A.M.: Ruth Anderson passes a man bent double beside the trail. Her stomach troubles having abated, she is once again a passer, not a passee. Battling rocky terrain on a moonless night, she is stumbling along at a breakneck four miles an hour. For just an instant, her mind wanders from her task—"Husband Johnny is sleeping now . . . pain in the right ankle . . . this flashlight is worth the extra weight . . . "—and suddenly she stumbles and nearly falls. Since the trail at this point is a steep downhill switchback, a mistake here could kill her. "Better concentrate on the footing," she thinks.

At "Rucky Chucky"—the American River crossing—there is an ABC camera crew lying in wait. She smiles at them and thinks, "They just want to see us up to our crotches in ice water."

The water level is in fact high enough to soak her shorts, so on the other side she ducks behind a bush and changes into a pair of long baggy pants that she has brought to protect her legs from poison oak. Though other runners look askance, it is the right decision. On the move once again, she begins to pass runners, many of whom are tied up with muscle cramps from the wet and cold.

Anderson, a self-described people-watcher, believes that particular habit has contributed greatly to her success. "I love to observe people who are successful," she says. "Watching Dwight Stones, I could tell he was a visualizer long before he became famous for it. He sees himself soaring over the bar before he actually does it. I try to use that same technique—I see the finish line, the cheering crowd, the aid station...."

Yet, she insists, she is not obsessively goal oriented. "I don't focus unwaveringly on the finish line. For me, running is not just a means to an end, but an end in itself. On the longer runs, I will set intermediate goals—like trying to reach a particular stretch of the trail when the sun is rising. It's nice to meet your goals, but I guess in my old age I'm getting more philosophical. Even when I'm not going very far or very fast, running is just a joy!"

A big part of that joy, she readily admits, has to do with the people she meets. "When I ran in Scotland," she recalls, "I met a man named Duncan McLean who was 92 and still running. Known as the Tartan Flash, his specialty was the 100 and 200 meters. He used to give demonstrations. He was beautiful."

Does Ruth see herself running when she is 92? "I certainly don't see myself quitting," she answers, laughing. "Hardly any of us quit. Even though I'm not as fast anymore, there are still lots of challenges. What keeps it fresh is the variety and the people. People may be the single biggest reason I run. Traveling all over the world to race, I've discovered that there's a common language among the folks involved in this sport. And runners cut across more lines than, say, tennis players. Of my two best running friends, one is a sculptress, the other a plasma physicist. They're total opposites—I love it!"

MILE 95, 8:15 A.M.: For Ruth Anderson and her pacer, Marty Maricle (race rules allow a pacer the last 40 miles), it's all over but the post-race Ranier Ale. Although she will finish well back of her goal of 24 hours, she will finish. And she will break the 30-hour barrier, earning another plaque.

In her mind's eye, she sees the finish line, the cheering crowd, the aid station, and such a vision lightens her step. When Maricle, who herself has won three silver buckles in prior Western States, tells Ruth that she is having trouble keeping up with her, she feels almost weightless.

Ruth credits her husband Johnny for much of her success. "I couldn't have done all I've done in running without the encourage-ment of friends and husband, particularly husband. Johnny is very supportive. He used to run with me, but he's had some injuries, and a weight problem, so he hasn't been running lately. Still, a lot of our life revolves around running. We can hardly plan a trip without directing it toward a race."

For Ruth, running has affected more than just her traveling habits. "It's made me a healthier person," she says. "I used to drink gin and tonics, but now they just don't taste right. I never used to like beer, but now I have to have my Rainier Ale after the race. My pulse has gone from 70 to 42, and my circulation is much better. Since I started my noon runs, I don't get sleepy in the afternoons anymore. One unexpected result: My sense of smell has gotten sharper. If there's a eucalyptus grove up ahead, I can smell it long before I see it."

The simple fact is, Ruth Anderson can't find anything bad to say about running; the sport has been good to her—and for her. She has almost miraculously escaped the orthopedic problems that plague so many endurance runners. She's had only two injuries that were serious enough to interrupt her training, and neither was due to stress. "One time in the Oakland hills," she remembers, "about a year after I started running, I was doing a nine-miler on trails. There was a people traffic jam, and in the confusion, my foot caught on a stump and I became airborne. The result was a dislocated shoulder; I grabbed it with my free hand and ran on, finishing third among women. After that, I became pretty well-known in racing circles."

MILE 100, 9:00 A.M.: With a victor's glow, Anderson crosses beneath the red-and-white finish banner at the Placer High School track. The vision that has sustained her for so long is firmly in focus. Though her time of 28 hours is slower than she hoped for, she feels satisfied. She thinks: "Better to have run and finished in 28 hours than not to have run at all." And in the eyes of the people who surround the finish line, the lady downing a Ranier Ale is a sure winner.

Well-known for her effervescence, Anderson is a perennial post-race favorite of the press. She is forever described in terms like "bouncy" . . . "effusive" . . . "exuberant." Indeed, nearly all the photos taken of her show a dazzling smile, perfect white teeth. It's enough to make one want to cry out: "Aren't you ever sad? Depressed? How can you always be so cheerful?"

She would answer that she is cheerful because she is genuinely happy. "I flat out love running," she says, making believers out of anyone within earshot. "Even my six-mile runs at noon are pure joy!"

The reporters gather around this second coming of Pollyanna, firing questions at her:

Q. The Western States is not the only ultra-marathon you run, is it?

A. No, actually the Western States is part of my Triple Crown. This year I've also done a 24-hour run in Santa Rosa and a 100-K run around Lake Merced in San Francisco.

Q. Isn't that the race that's named after you?

A. Yes, I hate to say it, but a lot of people are jealous about that one. (laughing) I guess when you get a race named after you, you're either a legend . . . or old.

Q. You don't look old. Is running a Fountain of Youth?

A. No, but it sure slows down the aging process. All other things being equal, sixty-year-olds will always run slower than fifty-year-olds. Except, of course, those other things are never equal. They've recently discovered that dedicated runners in their fifties are physically superior to sedentary 25-year-olds.

Q. Will you run the Western States again?

A. Yes, but I don't know when. That rascal is such a commitment—it really takes a whole year of training, and I'm not sure I'll have the time next year. I'll definitely be back though.

Q. So your goal of breaking 24 hours in the Western States is still alive?

Q. Oh, sure. But it's going to have to sit there for awhile. Now, if I could just find a way to overcome that nausea ...

Q. Ruth, did you ever doubt you'd finish?

A. No. Not even when I was the sickest. I was pretty relaxed before this run. Having already overcome something makes it a lot easier the next time.

Still fielding questions, Anderson makes her way to her white 1963 90S Porsche with a personalized license plate that reads SHRODR 1. "Someone beat me to SHROEDER," she explains. "It's named after the Peanuts character Shroeder—the one who plays classical music. Classical music is my constant companion on those long commutes from Oakland to Livermore. I turn up the music and have the loveliest fantasies. My husband Johnny gave me the Porsche as a reward for my working so hard to put him through vet school."

As Ruth starts to get into her car, a fellow runner hollers to her: "Hey, Ruth, where you going?"

"Home," she says. Then breaking into a huge grin, she adds, "The World Veteran Games are in Australia next year and I have to get started on my speed work."

KING OF THE ROAD

Runyon's Law: "The race is not always to the swift, nor the battle to the strong ... but that's the way to bet."
—Damon Runyon

JARAMA SPAIN, JULY, 1983: Kenny Roberts, 31, the "old man" of road racing, slows his 500-cc Yamaha motorcycle to 120 mph, leaning it through an S turn—left, right, left—with gyroscopic precision. The grace and rhythm of man and machine suggest a skier weaving around slalom gates. But for Grand Prix road racer Kenny Roberts, the speeds here are four to five times those of a slalom skier—added to which there is another racer hot on his tail.

A tick behind is Freddie Spencer, the brightest young star to hit international road racing since 1978 when Roberts arrived in Europe as a 26-year-old novice. Roberts, three-time world champion, is gunning for his fourth title; Spencer, the heir apparent to the Roberts dynasty, is after his first.

Out of the turn and onto a straightaway the riders accelerate to 165 mph, Spencer's nose to Roberts's tail. On the 19th lap, Spencer roars by Roberts; on the 21st lap, Roberts retakes the lead. The Spanish crowd, high on sunshine and red wine, cheers every pass, every parry, as if it were a bullfight.

Downshifting to second gear for a sharp turn—a "right-hander"—Roberts steers a slightly wider line than usual, and suddenly Spencer is by him on the inside. But he has too much speed for the curve and his front wheel starts to slide away from him. As Roberts whizzes by, he glances over at Spencer, now in a controlled skid, and sees that the kid, behind his plexiglass face shield, is smiling. And waving. Roberts shakes his head and thinks: It's amazing how much that kid reminds me of me.

Spencer, having righted himself, resolutely curls his gloved fingers over the throttle and sets out after Roberts. In 10 seconds he is going 150 mph. In 60 seconds he has made up the lost time and is once again staring into both barrels of the Yamaha's exhaust pipes.

They hold that pose for ten laps in perfect unison, like two banking fighter jets. On the 33rd of 36 laps, Spencer guns it by Roberts on the outside. On the last lap, Roberts, making his move, gets caught on a turn behind a rider being lapped, and Spencer wins the race by a few bike lengths.

On the rostrum, Roberts can't help watching Spencer, who is busy basking in the adulation of the crowd. While the Star Spangled Banner plays, he thinks, Yeah, Freddie's got it all: Young, cocky, fearless, always races to win ... he's the spittin' image....

Yet Roberts is vaguely disturbed by something. An idea has flashed through his mind, like a subliminal message on a movie screen. Over the next two months the idea will focus, and he will see its awful truth: "Freddie Spencer Wants It More Than I Do."

More than anything, it is the nagging presence of that idea than persuades Roberts to retire after the 1983 Grand Prix season.

MODESTO, CALIFORNIA, 1951: Kenny Roberts started racing when he was born, on New Years Eve, 1951. He was two weeks premature, which his parents forever blamed on a hit-and-run driver who sideswiped the family car when Kenny was still in his mother's womb. The result, in her words, was "an awful birth and a tiny baby." Some have argued that Roberts has been seeking revenge against bad drivers ever since.

As a boy, Kenny was small and loved horses, prompting those close to him to predict he'd become a jockey. "I was a cowboy," he says with some dignity. "I didn't want anything to do with motorcycles." When he was 12, the people he was working for bought their sons a mini-bike, but even then there was little hint of Roberts's golden future in motorcycle racing. "I just wasn't interested. I was a damn cowboy and had the hat and boots to prove it. But they kept pushing, and eventually I tried it. I can't say I took to it immediately 'cause I drove it right into a house trailer. It scared the living hell out of me . . . I guess that was all I needed to get hooked. That adrenaline ripping through you when you're scared is exciting stuff. I was determined to master that mini-bike. Within a couple of months, I'd built my own out of a bicycle frame and a lawnmower engine."

At the tender and illegal age of 14, Roberts began racing the dirt tracks of central California. He spent the weekends of his youth in San Joaquin Valley towns, growing bolder and better. His confidence was amazing even then. Everyone agreed: Kenny always looked as if he knew what he was doing.

By the time Kenny Roberts was 16, his name was known in Lodi, Turlock, Marysville, Fremont—wherever there were motorcycle people. He was winning everything, and had already established himself as the type of guy you either loved or hated. Some hated his aggressiveness, his disheartening habit of beating everyone; others loved those same qualities and came to the track in droves to watch him and get his autograph.

Unfortunately for the sport, lots of young men were quitting racing because they knew they couldn't beat Roberts. To instill competition, the race organizers began to handicap him, starting him behind the rest of the pack. Still he won.

The rules didn't allow him to turn pro until he was 18, but he never regretted his prolonged adolescence. "I wasn't ready before then," he says. "Motorcycles were just fun to me. I didn't have a career. I was working in a repair shop, riding around the irrigation canals with my buddies, having fun. Money didn't motivate me, having fun did. The faster I went, the funner it was. People were always sticking faster motorcycles in front of me and saying 'ride this,' and that was fun. . . ."

It was certainly more fun than school, where "P.E. was my best subject and I cheated enough to pass." When he quit high school to start racing for money, he weighed 110 pounds. Triumph Motorcycles refused him a pro contract because they thought him too small; but he turned out to be the best rookie in the country, dispelling any notions that he was too weak or frail to handle a 300-pound motorcycle. The boy had an undeniable, inexplicable feel for motorbikes. Besides, as he is quick to point out, bulk is no advantage when trying to go fast on a motorcycle. "You don't see any super-heavyweights racing bikes," he says. "Smaller guys, who are more maneuverable, make the best racers. You need good reflexes, and the quick muscle fiber of a boxer, but you also need the endurance to go 45 minutes full out. You never get to relax. It's especially hard on the legs, wrists and forearms...." Pointing to a muscle on the inside of his elbow, he flexes and the muscle bulges like a tumor. "The throttle muscle," he says. "It's way more developed in my right arm than my left...."

In the best of all possible races, the rider's body melds with the bike to become one terrifyingly efficient speed machine. But, as Roberts points out, that's an ideal that is seldom realized. "Of the two big mechanical elements in racing—the bike and my body—my body is more complicated, and I don't understand it as well. That's why I start paying it special attention as a race approaches. I start drinking lots of liquids—juice, Gatorade, even a shot of whiskey if it's not too near the race. Liquids loosen up the joints. I have a particular problem with my arms knotting up, so I watch for that. I try to feel everything my body is doing. It's got to be 100% responsive, because I'm out there making instantaneous adjustments to the situation.

"At least two weeks before a race, I start working out: running, playing racquetball, hitting the speed bag. Sometimes I use weights, but most of my training time is spent on bikes. I ride a mini-bike for reflexes, and, because it's so physically demanding, a motocross bike for muscles."

Despite evidence to the contrary, Roberts believes motorcycle racing is an aerobic sport. "Nothing gets your heart pumping like motor bikes," he says with childlike enthusiasm. "Not even Formula One race cars. If you crash in a car you're still in the cockpit, but if something goes wrong when you're on a motorcycle, you're going down. A meeting of you and the road." Roberts' eyes take on a faraway look, as if recalling his lost youth. "Yeah, I've sat in motor-homes all over the world with icepacks on my knees, elbows, shoulders...."

Although it would seem that he has the necessary size, strength and quickness to be a great motorcycle racer, Roberts believes the real key to his superiority lies in his nasty disposition. "I've always been very aggressive. As a kid, I was mean and stubborn. On the track that translated into a willingness to ride something even if it wasn't quite right. If they said it couldn't be ridden, I went out to show them they were wrong."

Roberts feels his first race demonstrated his naturally feisty nature. "I was riding a 50 cc clunker," he remembers. "It died on me not far into the race, and I got off and kicked it."

ON THE ROAD, CENTRAL CALIFORNIA, 1970: Eighteen-year-old Kenny Roberts sleeps in the back of the van, while his new manager drives south all night, reaching Ascot Park Race Track by dawn. As they pull into the parking lot, Roberts awakes, immediately remembering who he is and where he is going. He's Kenny Roberts and by god, he's going to show the world; he's going to be Grand National Motorcycle Champion.

They find a spot in the paddock. Setting up in the manner of a picnic, they lay out the bike, the tools and spare parts, then the fold-up chairs and cooler. It is home for the next two days.

It is also the Big Time, at least as far as Roberts's ice-blue eyes can see. It is the US Grand National Circuit. Pro ball. Twenty-five races in five different categories, from San Diego to New Hampshire. This Ascot Park race is called a "TT" event, which is a steeplechase with jumps and left and right turns; but a Grand National rider has to be able to do it all: the Mile, the Half-Mile, the Short-Track (quarter-mile), and the fastest and most dangerous event of all, Road Racing.

The sun goes down and the spotlights come on, highlighting everything in harsh incandescence. Roberts, dressed in red-and-white leathers and a blue-striped white helmet, leans on his handle bars, opening and shutting the throttle as a warm-up exercise. At the starter button, 30 forearms flex into action. The air is filled with the spray of sand and the throaty crackle of motor bikes. Roberts gets off well and is leading the race at the halfway mark. But then, suddenly, his front wheel hits a hole on Turn Four and he gets sideswiped and thrown from his bike. He doesn't fly very far, but he hits the track, rolls, bounces, flies up in the air again, hits a wall headfirst and crumples.

As he lies there, half conscious, dozens of reverberating motorcycles skid and slide within inches of his head. One of the other riders gets rattled and rams into Roberts's bike, sending the twisted machine flying over his prone body.

After that, Roberts quickly learned how to stay on his bike. In his second year as a pro, he won nine races, set several track records, and earned $50,000. Showing remarkable versatility, he became the first rider to win every type of race. He also became the first second-year pro to sign a contract with Yamaha. In his fourth season, at the age of 21, he became the youngest man to win the Grand National Championship, a feat which helped earn him more than $150,000.

HOUSTON ASTRODOME, 1975: Kenny Roberts, looking fit and trim in his tight yellow-and-white leathers, stands in the pit watching his mechanics tinker with the bike he will soon race: a 250 cubic-centimeter Yamaha TZ. God, how things have changed, he thinks. From a mini-bike with a lawnmower engine to Yamaha's latest proud beauty. She'll do 0 to 60 in about 3.5 seconds, which means more fun, more money, and I don't even have to get my hands greasy. Two full-time Yamaha mechanics do the dirty work.

Suddenly, there appear some bad-ass guys in beards, longhair, black T-shirts, shades and scars. They are in the stands, but at the Astrodome they can get right down next to the pits.

"Hey, Shorty," one of them hollers. "What's with the Nip crap? What ya got against American bikes?"

"Get a Harley!" another yells.

A third, too drunk to talk, heaves his beer can in the general direction of Roberts.

Having grown up in the heart of Hells Angels country, Roberts is familiar with the type. It is the one he believes gives motorcycling its bad name. Mention motorcycles to the average American and he immediately thinks of the Hells Angels, or Marlon Brando in "The Wild Ones." In other parts of the world, where cycles have long been an important means of transportation, the image is somewhat more benign. In Europe, for example, up to 300,000 fans attend Grand Prix Road-Races and motorcycle racers are elevated to the level of cult heroes. Here in America, the only cult heroes ride Harley-Davidsons. Mention Yamaha and you're likely to hear, "Yamaha?! What's that, some wimpy Chink brand?"

There's something besides Roberts's fancy foreign bike that bugs the hooligans, but they can't quite put their finger on it. Maybe it's his sandy-blond hair, too neat and tidy despite longish sideburns. Or his cocky air. Or the fact that he's so damn good.

The drunkest of the hooligans, feebly lobs another beer can toward the pit, but by this time Roberts, helmet on, is walking away to the starting line.

Forty-five minutes later, after he has set a new track record, two of the hooligans' girl friends approach Roberts for his autograph.

EUROPE, 1978: The 500 cc Grand Prix Championship, the most coveted prize in motorcycling, is a series of 12 road races held all over Europe. There, racing is more of an obsession than a sport. The crush of fans is often so great at Grand Prix races that TV monitors are set up outside the stadium for the overflow. The big thing is for the fans to come dressed as their favorite rider, and the paddocks and stands are crawling with Kenny Roberts and Barry Sheene clones in their leather best.

By the end of the 1977 season, Kenny Roberts was the most accomplished motorcycle racer in America. As two-time Grand National Champion, he had won, all-told, 28 National Championship races, more than any other man in history. Yet, surprisingly, he did not long for the loftier European stage. He was married to Patty Rapp, making more than $300,000 a year, and content. "I didn't want to go to Europe," he admits. "I was satisfied racing in America. Europe didn't mean shit to me. But Yamaha wanted me to go there, so I went."

At first, European racers paid no attention to Kenny Roberts. It normally took years to learn the sophisticated European courses, where speeds were frequently more than 180 miles per hour. An American dirt tracker, new to 500 cc bikes, with fewer than 25 road-races under his belt—he could not possibly be a threat. Or so they thought.

The "cocky young Yank"—as he was called—won three of the first five European races, blowing away the field in Austria, France and Italy. He went on to win the Grand Prix Championship, the first American to do so, and the first from any country to win it in his first attempt. The "cocky young Yank" was now "King Kenny."

Roberts has often thought about the reasons for his rapid ascent to World Champion. "For one thing I had the equipment and the experts. Yamaha is great for that. They teamed me with former world champion Kel Carruthers, who acted as my coach and manager. Then they added a few mechanics, plus two Japanese engineers who were responsible for improving Yamahas for next year—eight on the team altogether.

"The reason the Japanese dominate the motorcycle industry," Roberts adds, "is because they strive year after year to make the best bike they can. Meanwhile American companies just strive for profits. Every year I can count on the Yamaha being lighter, faster, better than the year before. And they haven't had a racing breakdown since 1982. That's because the whole bike, from clutch lever on up, is built in the same factory. It's not like a Formula One race car, where someone builds the brakes, someone else the chassis, someone else the motor components."

While Roberts is willing to give Yamaha their due, he is not the sort to underplay his own role. "One time I was standing with Mario Andretti," he says, "and the press asked him how much of his winning was the car and how much the driver. He said that auto racing was 90% car and 10% driver. Well, in motorcycles, it's more like 70% rider and 30% bike. The main reason I did well in Europe was my aggressive dirt track background. On dirt you learn what it's like for the bike to get out of shape—you accept a certain amount of sliding with the front end. The Europeans weren't into sliding."

Before Roberts came along, nobody in big-time European racing had ever deliberately slid a road-racing motorcycle. Nor had they ever dragged their knees on curves or hung their butts off their bikes, as is his habit. As he explains, "I do those things to lower my center of gravity. It reduces my chances of throwing the bike and allows me to play the all-important mind game. That's where I fool myself into believing that I'm going, say, sixty when I'm really going eighty. If you can slow the mind down, you'll do all right out there."

One of the many problems a rider faces trying to drive a motorcycle rapidly around a curve is the centrifugal force that wants to throw him and his bike to the outside of the bend. To compensate for this, the rider leans in. How far he leans in depends on his speed. Also on his experience and his nerve. Roberts, in the words of one observer, "ain't afraid to lean that mother over."

"It's a game of inches," Roberts says, "An inch too far and the bike scrapes the ground ... followed by them scraping you off the pavement. An inch the other way and you lose the race."

At first the other racers thought he was crazy, but his success soon provoked them to start copying his knee-dragging style, and it is now de rigueur among world-class racers. While most use knee pads to prevent the wear and tear of their leathers, Roberts continues to use super tape "because I can feel the road better."

Roberts's wife and their two kids toured with him that first season in Europe. The family drove from race to race in a roomy $35,000 motorhome, which allowed them to park in the paddock and be a part of the racers' community. "It beat the hell out of staying in hotels," Roberts says, "but it was still very tough on Patty. After a race it would take me a week to slow down enough to be able to eat and sleep normally. Then it would be time to get ready for the next race. It got to Patty and I couldn't help her.

"I'd spend hours thinking about the racetrack, my mind spinning out at 11,000 rpm's. I would mentally place myself there, on the motorcycle, on the track, racing against Sheene and Farrario and the others. That way I could make the right decisions once I got out there.

"You have to learn to filter the important from the unimportant, so that when you get pushed to your limit—even though you know you could die—nothing affects your concentration. This is the deal you make, this is what you do. You race motorcycles and you might die. It's exciting because you have to get it right. A good guess will not be good enough."

YAMAHA TEST COURSE, JAPAN, FEBRUARY, 1979: All alone on the track, Roberts hits the front brake and the new Yamaha YZR500 slows to 120 mph. He is approaching a fast right-hand turn that, as the Yamaha test rider, he has taken many times before. Maybe he is thinking of something else, or maybe the absence of other riders causes a letdown, because suddenly he loses control of his front tire and the bike slides out from under him, throwing him hard against a guard rail and knocking him out.

He has ruptured his spleen, fractured his left foot, and compressed the 11th and 12th vertebrae. He nearly dies, but the Japanese doctors operate on his spleen, put him in a couple of casts, and in three weeks send him home, telling him, "Oh-by-the-way, you'll never race again." He spends another week in an American hospital, then two weeks at home in a back brace so restrictive that he can neither bend nor sit.

When he returns to the hospital for X-rays, his doctors are stunned: his back has healed. Roberts, somewhat less stunned than the doctors, says he is glad because he is supposed to race in Austria in a few days. "Impossible," say the doctors. "Watch me!" says King Kenny.

Six weeks after his near-fatal accident, Roberts shows up in Salzburg, Austria. When he pulls on his leathers over his back brace, everyone realizes that he's come not just to watch but to compete. The press surrounds him, asking how can he do it, what if he falls, does he intend to ride as hard as before? He tries to explain: "Breaking my back is something for me to overcome, something to make me better. I plan to ride harder than before." Whereupon he does just that, winning the race by several seconds. A week later, he finishes second in Germany, followed by three straight wins in Italy, Spain and Yugoslavia, giving him a seemingly insurmountable point lead toward his second straight World Championship.

JARAMA, SPAIN, MAY, 1979: An irritable Kenny Roberts arrives in Spain. His back hurts—even though he is loathe to admit it—and he knows that Jarama, a short bumpy circuit with lots of hairpin and horseshoe curves, is hell on backs and shoulders.

When he checks in, he is met by a FIM (Federation Internationale Motocycliste) official, who gives him the bad news. "Senor Roberts," he says with a saccharine smile, "due to poor attendance, we must cut by one-third your appearance money. We hope you understand...."

Roberts is in no mood to understand. He knows that the appearance money scale, based on points scored the previous season, is immutable and obligatory. He also knows that he is tired of getting jerked around by race officials, most of whom are more concerned with their expense accounts than they are with the riders' problems. Consequently, there is a sharp edge to his voice when he says, "Your poor attendance is not my goddamn problem. It's right in the rule book that you have to pay me!"

The FIM officials, shocked by his profanity, refuse to speak to him after that. Roberts discontinues the protest, turning uncharacteristically silent, and the Spanish breathe a sigh of relief that the incident is over. Senor Roberts can be such an ungrateful peasant.

Unfortunately for those same solemn FIM officials waiting on the elevated rostrum, that "ungrateful peasant" wins the race. While Roberts makes his way through the throng—the backslappers, handshakers, cameras and notebooks—the old men in dark suits grow uneasy. As he climbs up to the rostrum, the American national anthem blares through giant speakers.

One of the solemn old men makes a speech, complete with congratulatory praises, all in Spanish, all ponderously translated. Then another official begins to guide a massive trophy towards Roberts, who, though smiling, seems to be . . . giving it back? What's that? What is he saying?

He says thank you, but he doesn't want it. Doesn't want it? No, he says he's sorry we don't have any money, and he suggests we melt it down and use the money to pay a couple of riders their appearance money. . . .

The crowd goes crazy, screaming and whistling and shouting. All manner of animal, vegetable and mineral debris begins to cascade down on the rostrum, and Roberts's crew hustles him back to the safety of his motor home.

It was a shot heard 'round the world of motorcycling. As a symbolic protest, it riveted the attention of his fellow riders. It marked the beginning of the Riders' Rebellion, a populist movement in a sport that was presumed to be too superstar-oriented to unionize. Roberts explains: "The FIM had always had the riders over a barrel. Because we had to race for the overall points, which earned us our money from Yamaha and Suzuki, the race organizers could pay us peanuts. I thought if I'm the world champion and getting peanuts, the other guys must be starving. I felt a responsibility."

The battle between the riders and the FIM came to a head in Belgium, where once again Kenny Roberts would be branded a troublemaker. "They had resurfaced the racetrack a week before the race," he remembers. "The pavement was uncured. Diesel fuel, which was used to keep the track from cracking, was oozing up to the surface. It'd be 2-3 weeks before it was right, and in the meantime, it was like riding on greased snot. But hell, the race organizers didn't care. They told us to race, we said no."

Roberts helped to organize a boycott. A maverick association was formed. The top racers threatened to start their own race circuit—called the World Series—and only when it appeared that they might pull it off did the FIM agree to negotiate. "Even then they tried to take my license away, to keep me from racing. Naturally they failed. It was a triumph of solidarity," Roberts says. "Prize money increased 300% and conditions got a lot better."

SILVERSTONE, ENGLAND, AUGUST, 1979: The crowd bursts to life when they spot Kenny Roberts returning to the starting line. Ordinarily, the mere sight of the world champion is sufficient to arouse their vocal zeal, but this is something special. An oil seal has just blown out during his warm-up lap, and moments before the start of a Grand Prix race, Roberts and his Yamaha 500 cc motorcycle are covered with oil.

With only seconds to spare, his mechanics get the seal pushed back into place and Roberts cleaned off. The mechanics worry that the seal won't hold up to the demands of a race in which bike and rider will exceed speeds of 170 miles per hour. And even Roberts— normally capable of total concentration—worries about the oil smears on his tires and handlebars.

Thirty riders on thirty bikes hit the first turn at more or less the same time, sounding like a swarm of angry wasps. Roberts is in ninth place, but that is not unusual. On the European Grand Prix circuit, the riders must push-start their bikes and Roberts, at 5'5" and 130 pounds, is not known for his fast starts. "I'm never first off the line," he says. "I always run a few feet farther than I really need to before dropping the clutch, because if I don't start the first time, those guys in the back row will be whizzing by me at 50 miles an hour."

By the twenty-mile mark, Roberts has caught and passed everyone except Englishman Barry Sheene, the local favorite. He is shifting through his six gears 55 times a lap, an average of once every three seconds for forty minutes. Suddenly, the Italian Virginio Ferrari drops out of the race. Roberts knows that this is the only man with enough points to deprive him of his second straight 500 cc World Championship; all Roberts has to do now to clinch the title is stay on the bike and cross the finish line. In other words, Play It Safe. But he can no more do that than fish can fly. It is indelibly etched in his character: he races to win.

Lap after lap, Roberts and Sheene ride knee to knee, wheel to wheel, trading the lead, antagonists in a two-man play. They know each other's habits well, these two, having battled to a one-two finish in the world the year before. Sheene has immense respect for Roberts and likes racing against him because he knows the American isn't going to do something stupid. Roberts admires Sheene's skills, but thinks the Englishman sometimes rides too conservatively, going for overall points rather than the win. Although Sheene finished second to Roberts in the 1978 point standings, he won few races. On this day, however, Sheene is riding aggressively, and Roberts knows the race will come down to the last lap.

As they roar into the second-to-last turn of the last lap, Roberts has a half-bike-length lead over Sheene. He has worked on this turn, perfecting the braking and gearing, and it pays off. He accelerates out of the turn, taking a full-bike-length lead into the short straightaway that follows. Approaching the last curve, Roberts realizes that there is only one way that Sheene can beat him; he must get inside Roberts. Kenny slows down earlier than usual, which accomplishes two things. First, it drives the impatient Sheene to the outside, where he must take a longer, wider line; second, it allows Roberts to accelerate earlier and come out of the turn faster, which he does. He takes the checkered flag a millisecond before Sheene. "When I crossed the finish line," Roberts remembers, "Barry's elbow was about stickin' in my ribs."

Everyone agreed that it was the greatest finish ever in Grand Prix Motorcycle racing. Besides the 100,000 people who saw it live, millions all over the world watched it on television. "For months after that race," Roberts says, "people who didn't know a damn thing about motorcycle racing were coming up to me and saying, 'Hey, aren't you that guy who beat Barry Sheene by a few feet in that fantastic race?'"

MODESTO, CALIFORNIA, NOVEMBER, 1985: Kenny Roberts, three-time 500-cc Grand Prix World Champion, sits behind the desk at his Yamaha dealership, remembering the highlights of a career that is not yet over. Sipping on his second cup of coffee of the morning, he says, "This year I only raced twice: Once at Laguna Seca, because I had helped build it into the biggest motorcycle race in America; and once in a eight-hour-endurance race that I did as a favor to Yamaha. The bike broke down after 7½ hours. If it had to break down, I wish it'd done it in the first hour. . . . If someone wants to pay me enough, I might race again. But they better start at fifty thousand dollars or we needn't even talk!"

Even in semi-retirement, Roberts is still a revered sports figure in Europe, Japan and parts of South America, where his fans buy 55,000 personalized Kenny Roberts Racing Helmets each year. In America, he is the prototypical unsung hero. "In the U.S. I'm just another guy," he says. "If I get out of Modesto, where I've lived all my life, I can walk down any street in America and nobody knows who the hell I am."

At 5′ 5″ and 135 well-toned pounds, Roberts looks fit and trim, although, he confesses, he is a couple of pounds over his ideal riding weight. He appears younger than his 33 years, despite the fact that his sandy hair is in a controlled retreat in front. His strong jaw and close-set blue eyes are perfect for the demeanor of stoic determination worn on race days.

But make no mistake, Roberts is a man who loves his fun. He likes to laugh, joke and drink with the boys. A child at heart, he recently broke his leg goofing around on a motorbike with his kids. "The most fun you can have on a motorcycle," he says, "is just riding around with your buddies or your kids."

You can also make heaps of money—and that's fun. Roberts earned more than a million dollars in every one of his six years on the Grand Prix circuit. Unlike most riders who rely heavily on prize money for their income, Roberts' contract with Yamaha has paid him for showing up and racing. "The purse has never meant that much to me, I preferred to be paid for my effort. For example, I lost out on the 1982 world championship because I ran out of gas on the last lap of a race that I was leading. It was a miscalculation on the part of one of the Japanese engineers. Now if I was paid only for results, I would've gotten nothing. My goal has always been to get fans to the race track and to ride as hard as I can. And I am going to ride as hard as I can, so why do I need a financial incentive? I don't like to lose—that's incentive enough."

Although Roberts has won races by going faster than other riders, he maintains that the thrill of riding a motorcycle lies not in phenomenal speeds, but in the mastering of technique. "There's more satisfaction in taking a 20-mph curve at 30, with perfect brake, gear and line, than in going 170 on a straightaway."

The average person, if placed aboard an accelerating 500-cc motorcycle (250 pounds, an incredible 150 horsepower), would die of fright long before it reached 170 mph. Yet Roberts, who has hit 190, suffered a blowout at 170, and broken his back at 120, maintains that he has never felt fear while riding a motorcycle. Excitement, yes; fear, no. "I've been nervous before a big race," he admits, "and worried about doing well, but that's not fear. And after a near miss, I've thought, 'Hey, I could've eaten it big time.' But then it's not fear anymore, is it? It's like slipping off a roof. While you're going down, you're too busy trying to save your ass. There's no time to be afraid."

At 33, he's still not afraid. And, furthermore, he adamantly denies that he has slowed up. "I can still go as fast on a motorcycle as I used to, but I don't want to." Clearly, he doesn't like the sound of that. "No, it's not that I don't want to go fast, it's that I don't want to put in the time necessary to get to the point where I can go fast. I gotta train for weeks before a race. It takes unbelievable concentration, and the brain gets tired."

Roberts readily admits that he has become domesticated. Recently remarried, his top priority these days is spending as much time as possible with his wife and three kids. "When I was racing the full season," he says, "I was away from home about 80% of the time. I'm not willing to do that anymore. I want to watch my kids grow up."

His oldest son, who is 12, is showing signs of wanting to follow in his father's tire tracks, a movement Kenny is trying to discourage. "I don't want my kids to race," he says with his usual directness. "It's a hard life and I don't want them to have to deal with the pressure of being Kenny Roberts's son. When my son bugged me about entering a race, I went out and bought him a set of golf clubs."

Roberts realizes, of course, that he can't stop his son from racing. "If he really wants to do it, he's going to do it. He is, after all, a Roberts."

A slender young man enters the showroom, demanding in a loud, friendly voice to see "King Kenny." He is dressed in motorcycle leathers and carries an official Kenny Roberts helmet. Roberts comes out of his office and greets the man, who pumps his hand vigorously and tells Roberts that he is his biggest fan. "I was in the army, stationed in Germany," he gushes, "and when I heard you were coming over there last year, I reenlisted just so I could stay and see you race."

"You're kidding."

They chat for a few minutes, with mostly the young fan asking questions and Roberts answering them. As the fan starts to go, he says, "Kenny, are you going to race in Europe next season or what? There's a heck of a lot of people over there that'd like to know."

"You know, son," Roberts says with sudden warmth, "It's just possible I might. I was just talking about that and, fact is, I might take a racing team over there myself. I just might...."

Back in his office, Roberts sits at an empty desk, wondering why he'd said that. He wasn't going back to Europe ... was he? He was going to stay in Modesto, be a Family Man, do something with his life besides race motorcycles ... but what? Not auto racing—he'd tried that and found it tame in comparison. And a guy could only play so much golf. No, nothing did it for him quite like motorbikes.

MOUNTAIN MEDICO

"Everest is a harsh and hostile immensity. Whoever challenges it declares war. He must mount his assault with the skill and ruthlessness of a military operation. And when the battle ends, the mountain remains unvanquished. There are no true victors, only survivors."

—Barry Bishop

A sudden cold wind swept down the south face of Mt. Everest, bringing swirling eddies of snow and ice. Peter Hackett, alone at 28,000 feet, felt his nerves tighten. He was standing on the edge of a sheer drop, staring up at a formidable barrier of rock and ice, a 900-vertical-foot fang that seemed to pierce the blue sky. He breathed rapidly through his mask until he could do it without gasping. Near the top of the world, it was what passed for "catching your breath." Although he could see the powdery plumes from countless mini-avalanches in the valleys below, all he could hear was the wind. He watched a bird, undoubtedly a Lammergeier with its long, narrow wings and diamond-shaped tail, floating effortlessly on invisible pillows of air.

He's having a much easier time of it than I am, Hackett thought, wondering what were the Big Adventures for birds? What did they do for kicks? For his part, he climbed mountains and studied the effects of high altitude on the body. Right now he was both subject and object.

Alone at great heights, he realized, there were contradictory pressures in play. On the one hand, he seemed raised to a higher

77

pitch of awareness. In the rarefied air, with no one to talk to, he tuned in with every fiber to the Voice of Nature. He identified with Her, felt intimate with Her. On the other hand, working at an altitude more than five miles above sea level created a mental numbness and a sapping of the will that could be fatal. Cowardice, it seemed, came easily at great heights: He could easily imagine himself just sitting down on the ice and becoming one with nature.

Admittedly, he wasn't much of an athlete as a kid: The kind who gets picked last for baseball, then shunted off to right field. His mother, who had given up a promising career as a concert pianist to marry his father, inspired him to take violin lessons, which he did for several years. Though he was better with a bow than a bat, he still lacked the tools of greatness.

The oldest of ten brothers and one adopted Bolivian sister, Hackett grew up in a strict Catholic household in the Chicago suburbs. His father was a physician, a general practitioner with a large middle-class practice that kept him away from the house for much of the time. As a young boy, Peter was cast in the role of surrogate head-of-household to an ever-growing brood of younger brothers. "So much is expected of the oldest child," he says. "I'm sure all that responsibility made me an over-achiever."

After graduating from Marquette in 1969, Hackett decided to go to the University of Illinois Medical School. Like his father he would be a doctor, but his motives ran deeper than a mere desire to follow in Dad's footsteps. As a teenager, he'd watched helplessly as doctors labored over his best friend, who had struck his head on the edge of a swimming pool. The friend died, and Hackett remembers wishing that he'd known enough to help.

As a college student in the Sixties, Hackett was appropriately radicalized by the times. He grew his hair long, dabbled in experimental behavior, and became attached to the notion that health care was a right, not a privilege. "I was committed to delivering health care to those who were normally bypassed by the medical establishment—that is, those who didn't have money. I didn't read Marx or Lenin and wasn't into the Daily Worker, but just like any student of my day I saw the inequalities. It was a time when you felt like maybe you could make a difference."

He interned at San Francisco General Hospital, a one-year stint that thoroughly soured him on the idea of a conventional urban medical career. "Every knifing and gunshot victim in the City came through there," he says. "I got sick and tired of all the violence." So the day after his internship was over, he fled to Yosemite Valley. He bought some hiking boots and dehydrated food, and went backpacking in the High Sierra.

After a couple of weeks in the wilderness, it dawned on Hackett that he had no desire to go back to the city. He asked at the Yosemite Rescue Center if they needed a doctor. "Never had a doctor," was the reply, "but can you teach an EMT (Emergency Medical Technician) course? We sure need one of those."

Although Hackett had never taught such a course before, he said he could do it and got the job. As there was officially no such position in the Park Service, he was hired as "Fireguard" at $4.47 per hour. In addition to teaching EMT classes, he participated in helicopter rescue missions.

"The whole summer was great," he says, as animated as he ever seems to get. "Before I started work in Yosemite, I went back to Chicago to see my family. My mother had recently died and my father was remarrying. After the wedding, I took eight of my brothers on a 212-mile canoe trip through northern Minnesota. The combination of Minnesota and Yosemite cemented my love for wilderness. For the first time in my life, I was working outdoors, doing physical labor, putting on muscle. I lived in a tent cabin in Yosemite and my next-door neighbor was an owl. I learned about geology, ecology, botany. I spent a lot of time in the Yosemite library reading up on soils, rocks and trees."

It was in Yosemite that Hackett was first introduced to rock climbing. He became friends with Beverly Johnson, the first woman to climb El Capitan, who taught him the rudiments of climbing. From the beginning, he was drawn to multiple-pitch routes. "It wasn't just getting to the top," he says, "I loved pitting myself against the mountain. Climbing is a sport that provides immediate results. Either you make the move or you don't. I also loved the concentration it requires. You can't be doing a move and thinking about work undone. And it's a sport that is essentially noncompetitive—there's no scoring system. It appeals to me as an individualist—plus it's done in a gorgeous setting!"

At the end of the summer, Hackett wrote his father that he wouldn't be returning to Illinois to become a partner in his medical practice. He had, he explained, found a home in the mountains.

Most climbers, at one time or another, dream of Everest. Even if they harbor no realistic hopes of ever seeing its slopes, let alone summiting it, the foreboding thought will visit them; they will find themselves, eyes closed in reverie, on Everest's icy slopes, testing their mettle against the harshest elements Mother Earth can conjure up. Unless they are among the few who will act upon this vision, the question will haunt them: Could I do it? When the crunch came, would I hold up?

Peter Hackett knew first-hand about that dream. And about Everest:

In 1852 a clerk rushed into the office of the surveyor-general of India shouting, "Sir, I have discovered the highest mountain in the world!"

The 29,028-ft. peak, located in the Himalaya on the Nepal-Tibet border, was later named for Sir George Everest, but the locals continued to call it Chomolungma, "Goddess Mother of the Earth." The yeti, or Abominable Snowman, half-human, half-ape, was said to inhabit the lower slopes.

From 1921 to 1952 eleven expeditions, mostly British, made serious attempts to put a man atop Mt. Everest, at the cost of ten lives. Although none of the expeditions succeeded, individuals climbed to more than 28,000 feet, doing the footwork and gathering the information that would be needed by the '53 expedition on which New Zealander Edmund Hillary and Sherpa Tenzing Norkay made the first successful ascent of Everest.

Peter Hackett first laid eyes on Everest in 1974. Mountain Travel, an adventure-travel organization, needed a trekking doctor for the summer. "They offered all expenses paid," he says. "It was an offer I couldn't refuse."

Three months later, when his job as trekking doctor was over, he was still in Nepal and out of money. So he worked on more treks, satisfied to just make his expenses.

It was in Nepal that Hackett was first introduced to Mountain Sickness. On his first trek to Everest Base Camp, he was amazed to discover that half of his group had flu-like symptoms: headache, nausea and vomiting. Only later did he realize that it wasn't the flu, it was Mountain Sickness.

During this time Hackett met John Skow, a Peace Corps volunteer who lived and worked in the Khumbu region near Everest. Alarmed by the number of deaths among high-altitude trekkers, Skow had finally convinced the trekking outfitters to finance a primitive medical clinic, which became known as the Himalayan Rescue Association.

Hackett was hired as the association doctor, or as he puts it: "I became the Himalayan Rescue Association. The clinic was a little Yak hut with a dirt floor, an open-pit fire, and a lot of chinks in the stone walls—one of those non-mortared little buildings the dust blows right though."

He still remembers his first patient: "I was having breakfast when the doctor of a group headed for Everest Base Camp dumped a guy off with me and said, 'The man has bronchitis and can't travel with us . . . we'll pick him up on our way back.' I said, 'Uh, okay,' but when I finished my tsampa and went out to check on him, I could hear the gurgling sound before I opened the tent flap. He had pulmonary edema. His skin was the same blue-grey as his parka. He promptly coughed up blood and went into a coma. I radioed for a helicopter, and two days later got a message back saying, 'The king is using the helicopter. Could you use something else?' The guy made it, though. He walked out of there."

Hackett used the yak hut for the clinic and at night slept in a tent in the front yard. The locals, good-humored Sherpas, loved having him around because he took care of them and their families, and because he made an effort to learn their language. They started slipping him food from the kitchens of the trekking groups. "God, the Sherpas are great," Hackett says. "They would carry extremely ill trekkers or Sherpas down to the clinic and I'd literally save some of their lives. The Sherpas would be so grateful that they'd give me a flashlight or a wool hat—something they knew I needed. The trekkers had no idea what kind of conditions I was living under. Finally I put up a sign: 'The doctor needs a new pair of pants,' or 'The doctor needs long underwear.'"

Winter arrived, closing out the trekking season. As usual, Hackett was broke. "At that time I didn't even know if I wanted to continue being a doctor," he says. "I was thinking of becoming a

Sanskrit scholar, of joining a Buddhist monastery, of getting into Tibetan medicine. Anything could've happened."

What did happen was that Mountain Travel once again offered him a medical job with a group trekking into the Karakorum, the Pakistani arm of the Himalayas. He describes his memorable journey to Pakistan: "I took third-class trains all the way, slept on the platforms with the beggars, had people die next to me during the night. When I finally made it to Pakistan and met the group leaders, they were appalled by the sight of their trip doctor. At that time I was probably about 120 pounds, with straggly long hair and a beard. I looked like a Hindu ascetic. The first thing they did was buy me a beer."

In 1979 word reached Hackett that there was to be an American Medical Research Expedition to Mt. Everest in 1981. It would be the first climbing expedition onto that mountain to have as its primary goal the collection of scientific data. Climbers were to be tested to measure the pressure of carbon dioxide in their lungs as a function of barometric pressure, which decreases as altitude increases. They would also be tested for MVO2, or maximum oxygen uptake. Their Hypoxic Drive to Breathe would be determined. Such studies would contribute greatly to the understanding of how climbers can perform work and survive at extreme altitudes, despite available oxygen that is less than one-third that at sea level.

When Hackett learned that John West was heading the expedition, he was anxious to go. "I knew working with scientists of West's caliber would be great. I also knew I was perfect for that expedition. I had lived at 14,000 feet. I spoke Nepali. And I knew the Sherpas. I offered the leaders my services, and eventually they agreed. I found out later they were hesitant because they thought I might side with the Sherpas on difficult issues."

There was reason to think so. Having spent five of the last six years in Nepal, Hackett knew and understood the Sherpas. But his appreciation for those short, sturdy mountain people was more than an intellectual one. As Medical Director of the Himalayan Rescue Association, he had spent most of a winter huddled around a pot-bellied stove with a Sherpa couple as his only company. He became close with the couple and later with their three children.

Returning to Nepal with the West expedition, he was shocked to discover that the couple had recently died. The story circulating in the village was that the mother, on her death bed, told the neighbors, "I'm not going to be around to take care of my children. Please make sure that Dr. Peter takes care of them."

Hackett searched for the kids as he trekked into the Everest base camp, finally locating them in the village of Khunde. As he describes it: "I found two of them in a second-story room about six feet by eight feet, with an open-pit fire and no bed. There was only one tiny window and it was very dark. I was flabbergasted. The boy was eight and the girl was ten. She was doing all the cooking; they were trying to make it on their own."

(Hackett located a better home for the kids and paid for their boarding and school. In effect, he became their adopted father. To this day, he visits them as often as possible, and continues to support them financially and emotionally. He intends to send them to college, if they want to go. And even though he's never been married, when he refers to them as "my kids," he makes it all sound perfectly ordinary.... "I'm having my 40th birthday party in Kathmandhu this year ... I gotta see my kids.")

As West predicted, Hackett's affection and respect for the Sherpas prompted him to take their side before the American Medical Expedition even got out of base camp. "I felt very strongly that we had a responsibility to put the Sherpas through some maneuvers, to make sure that they knew how to take care of themselves on the mountain. I talked the leadership into putting all of our Sherpas through a brief climbing course. Amazingly, we had Sherpas who had been on the mountain six times—some of them quite high up—but they didn't know how to use an ice axe, or didn't know how to stop themselves if they fell over backwards. At first the older Sherpas said, 'Oh, we don't need this, we've been on this mountain many times, we know what we're doing.' But it soon became painfully obvious to them that they never should have been up there without knowing the things we were teaching them. In the end, they appreciated the skills we helped them gain."

On September 1st, 1981, they started climbing the mountain. They made a route through the dangerous ice fall in three days—very good time—and established Camp II in six days. Camp III was also established quickly, but then progress was halted by the twin high-altitude bugaboos: bad weather and sick climbers.

It was well into October before Camp V (26,000 feet) was operational. In punishing winds teams of climbers eventually secured fixed ropes to the camp, but the camp itself remained defiantly inhospitable.

The first summit team went up and was buffeted down by the wind. Hackett was part of the second attempt, which got as far as Camp V. The first night they had three people and all of their equipment jammed into one tent because the other had been destroyed by wind. The second night they managed to put up another tent. But they weren't able to make an attempt on the summit because of a violent wind that nearly blew them off the mountain. The storm ripped open the tent doors and filled the tent with snow, totally burying their scientific gear and forcing them to retreat down the mountain.

Another summit team tried, but they too were blown off the mountain. With three summit teams repelled, it looked more and more like they weren't going to make it. Every time a team went up they consumed food and fuel and oxygen, which meant the upper camps had to be resupplied from lower down. The Sherpas were getting discouraged, and the climbers were beginning to think that maybe they had missed the window period between monsoon and winter winds. Supplies were running out. Morale hit bottom when the expedition got pinned down back in Camp II.

Although the scientific phase was going well enough, expedition leader John West still wanted to get somebody to the summit. He and John Evans, the climbing leader decided to pick the strongest people for a mad dash to the top. The strongest were Chris Kopczynski and Sherpa Sundare, who had summitted Everest in 1979. They also had to try to send a doctor with them to get some measurements. They decided upon Steve Boyer, who was a superbly-conditioned athlete, but who'd once already had pulmonary edema.

Off they went, going directly from Camp II (21,000 feet) to Camp IV (25,000 feet) to try to save time. Boyer came down with pulmonary edema again because of the fast ascent. He was able to descend on his own power, leaving Kopczynski and Sundare up there. At Camp II a big discussion ensued as to what to do: The consensus was that they still needed some measurements up high on the mountain.

Chris Pizzo, a strong climber, volunteered. He hadn't been bothered much by the altitude and was still in fairly good shape. But he needed somebody to go with him. Hackett had just come down a little while ago after getting blown off the South Col, and few climbers had ever descended from that height and then turned around and gone back up. But Hackett felt the same way as Pizzo, that they had to make a last-ditch effort. On the other hand, he had to face the fact that he had frostnip, was vomiting, had lost a lot of weight, and had bronchitis. Still, Pizzo needed someone to go back up with him and Peter knew that he was the last hope.

As Kopczynski and Sundare had done, Pizzo and Hackett and two Sherpas went straight to Camp IV without stopping at III. To their amazement, Kopczynski and Sundare were at Camp IV, having summited that afternoon. They had gone from the South Col (26,200') to the summit in 4 1/2 hours, a remarkable feat. However, unable to recover any of the scientific equipment buried at Camp V, Kopczynski had taken no measurements on the summit. Pizzo and Hackett felt obligated to push on and try to get those measurements.

The next day they moved up to Camp V and during the night they tried to do sleep studies with tape-recorded EKG monitors. But Hackett resisted sleep. Huddled in a fetal position in his sleeping bag, he experienced intense longings for things he couldn't have. He thought of lamb chops ... chardonnay ... Susan.... "Hypoxia at first sight," he mumbled, smiling sadly.

Arising at 2 am, they worked in the frigid darkness, melting snow for water, changing the batteries in the tape recorders, calibrating instruments and adjusting crampons. Gasping for breath as an icy wind tore at them, they worked slowly. In that extreme cold their muscles were rigid and unresponsive, and it was hours before they were ready to climb.

Then Pizzo realized that he had lost his ice axe when he abandoned Camp V during an earlier storm. Down lower on the fixed ropes he hadn't needed it; but above Camp V, where no such ropes existed, it was essential equipment. Ascending Everest without an ice axe was akin to a kayaker descending a whitewater river without a paddle.

One of the Sherpas had lost his axe too, so they decided they would go in two roped teams, one ice axe to a team. Chris and his Sherpa, Yong Tenzing, got off about 6:30 a.m. Hackett was having trouble with his crampons and didn't get off until 7:30 with Sherpa Nuru Zonbu, a young, inexperienced climber. About half an hour out of camp Zonbu stopped and said, 'Dr. Peter, my feet are freezing, I have to go back.' At that point it was very cold and windy. Thinking it might get warmer, Hackett convinced him to go on a little further. But 15 minutes later, he really got cold feet and said he would have to go back. Since Hackett would no longer have anyone to rope to, Zonbu took Hackett's climbing harness, as well as the extra bottle of oxygen and the rope, and went down.

At that point Hackett was physically doing well, but he was low on oxygen and it didn't look as if he'd be able to get to the top. He tried to catch up with Pizzo. Climbing rapidly, he wore himself out, then crouched behind a ridge to rest. The wind stopped and suddenly it was warm enough for him to take off his down parka.

But at 27,000 feet, stopping is not synonomous with resting. At that altitude, the body burns more fuel than it takes in, no matter what it's doing. It begins to live off its reserves, which are limited. Hackett knew he was fighting a war of attrition — on the losing side. Not wanting to totally deplete his reserves, he went on, climbing with slow, plodding resolve. He considered stopping to make a couple of scientific measurements, but decided it was more impor-tant to catch up with Yong and Pizzo. They needed another ice axe and Hackett needed the safety of roped partners. Besides he doubted he had the strength to do anything "extra." Just climbing and breathing were challenge enough.

As he was approaching the crest of the ridge, about 27,800 feet, he suddenly came upon the body of a dead woman in a narrow couloir. She was facing into the slope as if struck down in mid-climb, a frozen study, totally intact: clothes, boots, crampons. Doctor Hackett had seen a lot of dead bodies before, but this was the first time he'd ever had to climb over one.

Near the south summit he met up with Pizzo and Yong Tenzing on their way down. The Sherpa was leading. When he saw Hackett he said, 'What the hell are you doing here alone?' When Pizzo came down he had an ice axe. He'd found it a couple hundred feet below the woman's body. It had probably been hers. He told Hackett that when he picked up the ice axe he knew that he was going to make it to the top. He called it divine providence that an ice axe materialized out of nowhere at 28,000 feet on Everest.

They discussed whether or not Hackett should try to go for the top. He knew it would be dangerous, but the weather was fine and he was going okay. Pizzo assured him that the route up to the Hillary Step—the most difficult part between the South Col and the summit —was in pretty good shape. Then he looked at Hackett and asked a question that needed no answer: "When's the next time you're going to be this close to the summit of Everest?"

Hackett dumped some excess gear from his pack, forgetting to take out the two and a half pounds of frozen water. He and Pizzo each took a dexedrine tablet in hopes of increasing alertness and allaying fatigue. Pizzo assured him that he'd wait for him down at the old Camp VI site.

It was 2 o'clock in the afternoon and still a fine day: windy, cloudless, with good visibility. Hackett swapped Sherpa Tenzig his two-thirds full oxygen bottle for his own nearly empty one and took off. For the first time in his life, he thought he might actually get to the summit of Mt. Everest.

When he neared the south summit, a cold wind reared up. Hackett ducked in behind a ridge and slipped on his parka. Huddled there against the wind he thought to himself, "God, I could just hide here for a little while, then go down and say that I made it, that I summitted Everest." He was abruptly awakened from that dishonorable thought by the realization that if he stayed there he'd freeze to death.

He started moving again. The path from the south summit to the main summit was there before him. He thought it was the most beautiful ridge he'd ever seen. Very narrow, vertical on the Tibetan side and extremely steep on the Nepalese side. The most ominous-looking feature was the Hillary Step, a formation of rock and snow about 40 feet high and 80 degrees steep. It was the main technical barrier near the summit.

Moving slowly along the ridge, steadying himself against the wind, he was meticulous about the placement of his ice axe and his feet. One fall and it was all over.

He reached the bottom of the Hillary Step, gulping air like a man dying of thirst gulps water. When at last his eyes and mind cleared, he stared at the formation before him, awestruck that something so difficult was so close to the top. This was supposed to be the easiest route up Mt. Everest, but facing him was a very difficult section of climbing. It was only 40 feet long, but if he fell, he would bounce and roll all the way to base camp, two vertical miles below.

Seeing tracks starting up the Step, he tried to go that way. But the snow wasn't consolidated. It was very sugary and wouldn't hold the weight of a bird.

Then he saw tracks going over to the left, where it wasn't as steep and where there was some rock. He found better footing and began to climb. He still had his crampons on, but couldn't stop to take them off because his fingers couldn't function in the extreme cold. He could see sparks flying as the crampons scraped the rock.

Near the top there was a big boulder and a little ledge with snow on it. He had to put both his hands up on the snow and hope that the whole precarious piece wouldn't slide off into oblivion. Clawing the rocks madly with his crampons, he pushed himself up and flopped onto the top of the boulder, like a beached fish.

For awhile he just lay there hyperventilating. At this point he realized that he had made a total commitment. He would either get to the top or die. Then it occurred to him that he might get to the top and still die.

Progress was painfully slow: Take two steps, stop, lean over the ice axe and breath twenty times. He would come to a high point and think, "This is the top," but it was only a cruel visual trick of nature. There would be another high point, then another, and each time Hackett would be fooled. Yet somehow, through the pain and the disappointments, there was discipline. While the shrieking wind pummeled him, he plodded on, a leaden body encasing a flickering spirit. At this altitude, there was no style to his climbing, only willpower. Finally it was down on all sides: he was on top.

The actual top was a tiny plateau about three feet wide by six feet long. It was scary standing on that windswept piece of snow; but of course he had to do it because it meant standing on top of the world. He was higher than any earth-bound human. A wonderful feeling of fulfillment washed over him. Visibility was ... amazing —it seemed to approach infinity. He took pictures to prove that he had been there. Then he said a little word of thanks to the mountain for letting him get up, and prayed that she would let him go safely down.

Total time at the top: Fifteen minutes.

SNOWMASS, COLORADO, AUGUST, 1987: Dr. Peter Hackett is speaking before the Wilderness Medical Society, an organization of mountain men and wilderness doctors that he helped found.

"Acute Mountain Sickness shows extreme and unpredictable individual variation.... It can come on and kill in a very few hours, and if you're genetically predisposed to getting it, no amount of training will prevent it.... Specific maladaptions like pulmonary edema and cerebral edema are really a matter of poor water handling by the body ... water getting to places it shouldn't...."

Outside magazine recently ranked Hackett among the "Fifty Who Left Their Mark," calling him "the principal authority on the mysterious, deadly ailments that afflict high-altitude alpinists." The audience is extremely attentive to Doctor Hackett, who besides being the preeminent expert in his field is an articulate, thoughtful speaker. But it staggers the mind that this man has summitted Mt. Everest. He appears so ... well, ordinary. He certainly appears to lack the indominatable vigor necessary to summit Mt. Everest. Dressed casually in blue jeans, Nikes and a canvas shirt, he is slight of build, 5' 10", 150 pounds. With Brillo-pad hair and a scraggly beard, he looks to be more scientist than climber.

After his lecture, he moves to an outdoor cafe for lunch, where he speaks informally about his life on and off the mountain. As he approaches his fortieth birthday, he says, he is a more temperate person than he once was. Though proud of his climbing accomplishments, he sees, perhaps with greater clarity than ever before, that he has been lucky. "So many of my friends who have been killed climbing have had more skill than I have," he says.

"In most cases it was just bad luck. Being at the wrong spot at the wrong time. One of the two women with us on a recent hang-gliding expedition to Everest—the one with the best chance of becoming the first American woman to summit Everest—was just killed a month ago on Mt. Logan. A cornice fell off taking her with it ... now, there's no way to have predicted that."

Despite a greater appreciation for his own fragile mortality, Hackett is not yet a member of the staid milk-and-cookies set. "I still do, and will always, spend time on mountains. Chris Pizzo is arriving tomorrow and we're going climbing. I'll always maintain a skill level that will allow me to survive and enjoy it out there...."

Just then a sleek young blonde in an electric-blue halter top strolls by and Hackett's eyes follow her, his voice temporarily trailing off into a distant monologue. "You know," he says sadly, after she has passed, "there are about 300 beautiful women here for every one in

Anchorage, where I live." Then smiling wryly: "Yeah, I have a tendency to be self-destructive if I stay too long in an environment like this. It's a lot healthier for me in the wilderness."

That helps to explain Hackett's willingness to fly into a base camp on Mt. McKinley every spring, set up his portable lab at 14,000 feet, and live there for the two-month (May/June) climbing season measuring the blood oxygen level of prospective climbers. "That's the essence of what we need to know to determine how well a climber has acclimitized, how well his lungs are working. If he tests low, I'll tell him that he should stay down another couple of days. He can, of course, do whatever he wants, but at 14,000 feet on McKinley he'll tend to believe me. At sea level, he might be a bragging fool, but up there it's 'Doctor Hackett, would you check me out and tell me whether I'm adjusting okay.' "

Hackett can measure acclimitization all right, but he admits there is no sure-fire way of predicting whether someone will make it to the top of the mountain. Extreme altitude causes physiological stress for everybody, but with varying degrees of intensity. Ironically, Hackett refers to altitude as the Great Equalizer. "Someone who is not necessarily a great athlete at sea level may do very well at high altitudes. A good predictor is the Hypoxic Drive to Breathe, which we can measure in the lab. We make the subjects hypoxic (under-oxygenate their tissues), then see how much breathing it stimulates. On our expedition, the three non-Sherpas with the highest hypoxic drive were Kopczynski, Pizzo and me, the same three who made it to the top."

Besides the physical skills, however, one must factor in the intangibles like drive, judgment and experience. "I'm a perfect example," he says, "I don't know how I made it to the top of Everest. I wasn't supposed to. I was emaciated, vomiting, with bronchitis and a broken rib from coughing so hard. But at some crucial point, I made a commitment."

In climbing—perhaps more than in any other sport—it is that ability to commit that predetermines success. Austrian climber Reinhold Messner—who in 1980 soloed Mt. Everest without the aid of oxygen and is generally regarded as the world's greatest climber— tests only slightly above average in the lab. "He's been climbing since he was about four," Hackett says, "so he certainly has the experience. He's technically superb, knows his limitations, takes well-calculated risks and is highly familiar with the environment.

Well-calculated risks? Like soloing Mt. Everest without oxygen? "For Messner it was," Hackett insists. "On the other hand, Roger Marshall, who tried it and died, probably thought the same thing."

From the top of the Hillary Step, Hackett looked down and didn't know what to do. His first thought was to jump, but he realized that he would have to land on an angled slope and the chances of breaking an ankle were good. Alone, 5 1/2 miles above sea level, a broken ankle would be fatal. He didn't want to down-climb the side he'd come up, because if he fell, a not unlikely prospect, there would be no stopping. He considered going down the Tibetan side, but that too was nearly vertical.

There was only one thing to do: turn around into the slope, face into the crumbling snow, and try to kick his way down one step at a time. With full realization that he might fall, he tightened his pack and made sure his oxygen bottle was secure. Then he checked his gloves and oxygen mask. Turning into the slope, he kicked the first step down, kicked the second step down. . . . He planted his ice axe in front of him and suddenly all three points of contact broke loose and he started falling.

"I remember my thoughts very clearly. I'll never forget them. First was, 'Oh, my god, I'm falling. This can't be happening. Now is not the time for this to happen.' Second was, 'It's unbelievably easy to die. I'm not even going to feel any pain.' Third thought was, 'Holy cow! I've stopped falling. I'm not dead.'

"I was hanging upside down from my knees, with my lower legs wedged behind a flake of rock. Facing away from the mountain, I was looking down towards Camp II, a 7,000-foot drop. At that point an incredible will to survive took over. I don't know what else to call it. All my reactions became very automatic and extremely sharp. I had to get upright, and to do so I had to sink my ice axe into a little crack in the rock above me and pull myself up. This involved a series of exhausting situps. Each time I bent forward I would try to wedge the blade of my axe into a tiny crack. After each failure, I gulped air for several minutes. Finally, the ice axe stuck.

"I pulled myself up and there in front of me, where I had made a hole in the snow from the fall, was a fixed rope from a previous expedition. It was two feet under the snow. I grabbed onto it and was able to lower myself until it went under some ice. I fell again, but only a few feet this time, landing upright, feet stemmed against rock on one side and ice on the other. The rope was exposed again at that spot and I was able to get to an 18-inch ledge at the bottom of the Step."

By this time, Hackett was totally drained. He didn't know if he had the energy to make it back. It was about 4:30. The sun was low and it was getting colder. He had to make it back to camp or die. He had no bivouac gear, no stove, just one frozen water bottle.

To retreat via the south summit meant going uphill again, but Hackett knew if he tried to do that, he'd collapse from exhaustion and freeze to death. He decided his best chance was to go out on the Tibetan side and traverse around the mountain. It was steep and there was lots of loose rock and snow. When he finally made it to the other side, he was nearing his physical and emotional limits: He imagined that he looked like a dying animal.

Then Pizzo, who had been waiting at the old Camp VI site, saw him. He'd been there three hours in deteriorating conditions. He had run low on oxygen, but had found a cache of bottles abandoned by a previous expedition, one of which had a little oxygen left.

"It was a real hero's move," Hackett is fond of saying "If he hadn't waited, I might never have made it. Chris Pizzo and I will be friends for life. Cameraderie is a big reason that I climb. My companions mean everything to me. I'll never again hire on with a group of people I don't know. Climbing mountains provides a unique combination of solitude and deep companionship.... I usually feel lonelier in Anchorage or San Francisco than I do in the wilderness. In the city, there's the alienation. In the mountains I feel intimate with the forces of nature. It's a very spiritual place for me."

When Pizzo got on his radio to say that Peter had made it, everyone at Base Camp was tremendously relieved. They all thought he was dead, which was a notion that had crossed Pizzo's mind as well. He'd already made a tape that said, "This is Chris Pizzo speaking. If you find this tape it means that I have perished. On this tape is some very important data. I was waiting for Peter Hackett when it became clear that he must have perished up above. I am leaving this tape because my chances of survival are also very slim...."

Hackett and Pizzo made it to Camp V that night well after dark, startling their Sherpas who had also given them up for dead. A few days later they were in Base Camp. And a few days after that, having finished their experiments, they were moving down the mountain. As they approached the first villages, the Sherpas came out and greeted them with gifts and chang (the local brew). For Hackett it was "local boy makes good." Emaciated, bronchitis, broken rib, and frostnip in his fingers and toes that would plague him for the next six weeks; still, he was a happy man.

Peter Hackett was the 111th person and the 11th American to stand atop Mt. Everest, and the first to solo from the South Col. Yet such a distinction has brought little financial reward. Nor is there much money in his high-altitude research. Consequently, Hackett works in the Anchorage emergency room to finance his other pursuits. Although he's not that fond of Anchorage, he's willing to put up with its weather, its isolation and its dearth of female pulchritude in order to pursue his goal of doing clinical research on climbers who get sick. Although no stranger to loneliness, he thinks more than ever about getting married, while admitting that it takes a pretty remarkable woman to keep up with him. "The world is not bursting with women who want to take their honeymoon on Mt. McKinley."

He is often asked why he wasn't felled by Mountain Sickness on Everest? Why was he able to make it to the top when so many others have failed? "For one thing," he admits, "I was lucky, because in addition to a high Hypoxic Drive to Breathe, you need big-time luck to succeed on Everest. You need, above all, good weather and good health. The meterological moods of Everest can be vicious. The South Col, where merciless winds blow furiously all the time, is one of the least hospitable places on earth. Swirling snow often reduces visibility to near-zero. The extreme cold of Everest has cost many climbers their fingers and toes, and eighty-two have died challenging it."

There is no question that Hackett's decision to go to the top of Everest was a courageous one; but was it foolish? "I don't think so," he says. "I was going well and the conditions were perfect. There were risks, of course, but a life without risks is a life hardly worth living. Taking risks reaffirms the joy of living. Every time I've taken a risk I've come out of it with a stronger feeling about being alive. It's that reaffirmation of life that makes climbing so refreshing, so rejuvinating. Living on the edge—the narrow line between life and death—it improves everything in life. And as we say in climbing: 'The higher you get, the higher you get.'"

WINGED WONDER

"Can any sport be more exciting than flying?
Strength and adroitness, courage and decision, can
nowhere gain such triumphs...."
—Otto Lilienthal

Few people ever get the chance to be at the launch site of
a new sport the way Jan Case did with hang gliding. Her familiar-
ity with the sport began in 1969 when she met a man named Jeff
Jobe at a ski resort in Washington. He told her of his new
passion—ski kites, huge airfoils you hung onto while snow skiing
or being towed behind motor boats. Case immediately branded it
"crazy."

She and boy friend Lee Sterios saw Jobe again in 1972 at a ski
show in San Francisco. He was there displaying his kite, and he
told Case that people were jumping off of Southern California
cliffs with those things. Case and Sterios thought it sounded like
the natural summer sport for seasonally abandoned ski areas.
"You'd ride the ski lift up the mountain," she says, "then glide
down. We thought it was an idea that was going to make us a
million dollars."

After an all-night brainstorming session, a business was born.
Some Denver friends agreed to finance the project if Case and
Sterios would do the book work. So they moved to Denver and
spent the next few months doing research, writing proposals and
putting together a marketing idea. As a direct result of that work,
Chandelle Sky Sails was established to manufacture and sell sky

sails (or hang gliders, as they came to be called). They also started a school to teach others how to fly the contraptions. Although the idea of turning ski schools into "sky schools" never caught on, Chandelle prospered, becoming for a time the largest hang-gliding shop and school in the U.S. "I knew how to sew," says Case, "so I made our first sails. Later on, I had 16 people working for me. I was running a school seven days a week, selling, repairing gliders and taking care of the books. My main job, though, was to teach people how to fly their new gliders."

The irony was, Jan was teaching others how to fly before she herself had ever been aloft. She was telling beginners how fast to run on takeoff to produce proper lift for that day's wind currents, how far to ease the triangular control bar inward to achieve flight, how to stall in preparation for a smooth two-feet-on-the-ground landing—all before her two feet had ever left the ground.

Ironic, yes, but not illogical, says Case. "I can coach juggling," she points out, "even though I can't juggle three balls. I'm able to look at things, see dynamically what is going on and explain it. I'm a teacher."

Jan likes to say that love of flight is "in her blood." Her father was a Navy pilot who took her to lots of air shows. She credits her mother with allowing her "to be who I wanted to be." As a kid in Seattle, she was a tomboy. "I was skiing with my Dad and two brothers when I was four and waterskiing by the time I was eight. I was also into canoeing and sailing. . . ."

When she was 15, her brother brought home his Navy buddy, Lee Sterios. "He came for a visit and stayed a year," says Case. "He was 20 and like a big brother to me. When he moved out he told my mother he had to leave before he got someone in trouble, meaning me. Two days after I turned eighteen, he showed up at my door."

They had some good times and then Sterios told Case, "I love you, I will marry you, but first you need to grow up. Go to college, have some experiences. . . ."

Case took his advice, went off to Western Washington College in Billingham, Washington. It was there that another of her life's ironies revealed itself: she loved teaching but hated school. "It was 1968," she says, "and there were other things to do besides attend classes." While in Washington, she became a certified ski instructor and Water Safety Instructor. "I discovered I loved being around people when they were learning and recreating. When people are learning a new sport, they're the best of who they are. They do dream-like things. They bring a sense of adventure to sports that they don't bring to the rest of their lives.''

In 1969, diminutive Jan Case (she had topped out at 5′ 0″) quit school and found interim work in Seattle as a secretary. Predictably, she was soon fired. "I had the world by the tail," says Case with an engaging smile, "just the world didn't know it yet." She taught skiing that winter and in the spring called Lee to tell him she had grown up.

When Case went to San Francisco to be with Sterios, she found him driving a taxi cab and chasing women. At a stocky 5′6″ and 160 pounds, with a size-13 foot, he was not cut in the mold of the classic leading man: yet he had an appreciation—a passion—for women, which they returned in kind. Case's own pilot light—ever-burning— glows brighter when she speaks of Sterios: "He grew up on the Avenues in San Francisco, a surfer, a skier, one of those 'can-do-anything' kind of guys. Super-coordinated, but lacking finesse. Intense, strong. An extensive reader—everything from sci-fi to the classics. When he got into reading on the History of Flying, that became his latest and greatest passion.''

After they moved to Colorado and opened Chandelle, Sterios pursued flying with characteristic intensity, and by 1973 he was one of the top hang-gliding pilots in the country. "In the early Seventies," says Case, "that meant he could take off at will, control the glider so it would take him pretty much where he wanted to go, and land on his feet most of the time."

This assessment was from a woman who herself still hadn't flown. When people asked her "Why?" she'd mumble something about the 50-pound gliders being too big for her 95-pound frame. But when her friends and co-workers at Chandelle Sky Sails built and presented Case with her very own 32-pound glider, she knew the day of reckoning was near. "They shamed me into it," she says. "On the one hand, I felt a glow of pride, of acceptance; on the other hand, there was the terror: 'Oh, I've got to go up in this thing.' I realized that I was 22 years old and everything I knew how to do, I had learned as a kid. For the first time in a long time, I felt fear. There is a difference between butterfly stomach and scared shitless—I was the latter.''

For several days she did nothing more than hang in a harness tied up in the shop. Then she began lugging the glider around, trying to make friends with it. Finally, one day she set it up. She readied herself to fly, and then the wind switched. Somewhat relieved, she packed it up, walked to the other side of the mountain and set up again. But before she could get off, the wind switched again. She made five or six such trips, then spent the rest of the afternoon sitting under her wing, waiting, thinking, fighting panic.

"Finally," she says, "the fear of failure won out over the fear of getting hurt, and I am very afraid of getting hurt. I woke up one morning just knowing I was going to fly." She and Sterios drove to Green Mountain, ten minutes outside of Denver, and this day, unlike previous ones, she accepted his offer to carry her glider. "In the past, I'd been so tired after carrying the glider uphill that I wasn't worth anything. And I knew the most dangerous time in sports was when you were tired and had slow reflexes. So I put feminism in the closet and let Lee carry my glider."

On the way up the hill, Sterios acted as though he didn't care in the least if Case flew or not. He repeatedly reminded her that it was her decision, that she had nothing to prove, that she didn't have to fly at all if she didn't want to. "He was giving me every chance to bail out," Case admits.

At the top of the hill her mind was swarming with questions, but she knew that it wasn't more information she needed. More like Right Attitude. She took a few deep breaths and shook loose her muscles. Lee helped her strap on her harness, a 4-inch webbing that went around her hips and over her shoulders like suspenders. As it was before the days of state-of-the-art equipment, Sterios tied her onto the glider in the prone position with heavy ropes and elaborate knots. "Is that going to hold?" she kept asking, but he didn't answer. She slipped on leather gardening gloves—two sizes too big—then, because the gloves prevented fine motor control, Sterios strapped on her hockey helmet for her. He kissed her on the cheek, whispering a last vital bit of advice: "Have fun."

With that he was gone, running down the hill and yelling like a madman, heading for the bottom to help guide her in for a safe landing. "I was left alone at the top and it was loooonely," says Case.

Green Mountain was essentially a moonscape, devoid of significant vegetation, excepting one lone pine tree halfway down the slope. Case stared at that tree, then jerked her head away, riveting her attention on Sterios below. She was familiar with the phenomenon known as "object fixation." One tree on the entire mountain and a few weeks ago a friend had flown right into it. You should look at what you want to hit, not what you want to avoid, lest you create a self-fulfilling prophecy.

Finally, with somewhat less than total resolve, she crouched low and hoisted the glider onto her shoulders. She stood mannequin still, staring down at Sterios. "Looks good!" he yelled. "Go for it!" But she didn't go for it—not yet. She just stood there. Then she remembered what Lee had said: "Don't lift it till you're ready to fly." Obediently, she put it back down.

Three or four minutes went by. Then, when thought had ceased and only instinct remained, she picked up the glider and pounded down the hill. "I was going to show the ground I could really run hard," she recalls, "but in about four steps I was airborne." An acute rush of exhilaration ("Whoa, I'm flying!") was immediately overwhelmed by an equally acute rush of fear as she realized she had gone off a hill that was too high. She was, literally and figuratively, over her head.

The flight was a combination of slo-motion and hyper-speed. It lasted 10-15 seconds, but seemed like both a lifetime and an instant. As she rushed to meet the ground, it occurred to her that she didn't really know what she was doing. She had always told her students, "The hardest thing for people to learn in motion sports is how to stop," and now she herself was at that very decision point. What, she fought to remember, came next?...

Too late! The first thing to touch down was the bottom of the control bar, which caused the nose to dip and Jan to tip. She fell on her head, toppling over like one of those plastic ducks that bobs for water, popping the rivets on her hockey helmet. "The whole thing was so abrupt," she recalls. "Slam!-experience over!" She was dazed and dizzy, but otherwise unhurt. Immediately, she was assailed by a tangle of contradictory emotions: ecstasy, panic, gratitude, doubt—all at once. She thought, "I can't wait to do that again . . . I never want to do that again. . . ."

"Can't-wait" won out. "There was a strain of ego that said, 'My God, I can do anything they can do.' The guys at Chandelle were super—building training wheels for my glider, even constructing triangular pillows to protect my pelvis on belly landings—but when they'd get up on the mountain to help me fly, there was just too much emotion. They liked to tell me it was a 'go for it' kind of sport, and when I had trouble picking up the kite, they'd say, 'Just do it! Just pick it up!' So I'd pick it up and, lacking the technique needed to use the natural lift of the air, I'd be worn out almost immediately. What they didn't understand was that just holding it up took absolutely everything I had. They'd get so mad tears would fill their eyes, then I'd end up crying too. Teaching aviation is too tense; it's not the sort of thing you should do with loved ones."

Even to the majority of people who haven't the guts to do it themselves, hang gliding looks like a darn good time. One can easily imagine Early Man stopping and marveling at the graceful magic of avian flight. Myths deeply rooted in ancient civilizations speak of human flight. The idea is mentioned in Aztec and Chinese myths, as well as in the Bible, but what really captured human imagination was the tale of Icarus and his father Daedalus. Father and son, according to Greek mythology, were imprisoned on the Isle of Crete. Daedalus, being good with his hands, wrought two pair of large, plumy wings from the materials at hand, and the two flapped their way out of prison. Once aloft, however, Icarus began to grow giddy; he flew higher and higher until the sun melted the wax that secured his feathers, sending him to a watery grave. Daedalus, who has never gotten the press he deserves, flew safely all the way to Sicily, where he retired from flying.

By focusing attention on Icarus instead of Daedalus, the public has maintained an image of hang-glider pilots as hedonistic nitwits. The Icarus myth was detrimental to human flight in another way, too. It helped to reinforce the notion that human-powered flight depended on man emulating the flap-flap-flap of birds. The concept of merely gliding with the wind—an authentic bird-like concept as well—was alien to pre-19th century aeronautical thinkers. Leonardo da Vinci had the flapping-wing fixation, as did the Tower Jumpers of the Middle Ages.

So, at first, did Otto Lilienthal, now considered the "Father of Hang Gliding." One summer night in 1861, Otto and brother Gustav sneaked away from their home in the German province of Mecklenburg. Finding a military parade ground, they donned primitive wings of beech veneer, then spent the night running and flapping, flapping and running, until they dropped from exhaustion.

As a student at a Berlin technical school and later as an engineer, Otto continued to study aerodynamics. He also began to scrutinize the musculature of various birds, hoping to translate the intricacies of flapping wings into theories applicable to human flight. For years he clung to the traditional concepts of movable wings, until he eventually calculated that a 160-pound man would have to have pectoral muscles four-feet thick in order to duplicate the flapping motion of birds.

By abandoning the idea of movable wings, Lilienthal was finally able to focus on the act of gliding. He began to experiment with wings of rigid, curved surfaces. He constructed a hill near his home, took his experiments to the air and wrote scientifically about them. He was almost certainly the first person to gain altitude—to soar—thus earning him the title "First Birdman." In all, he flew safely 2,000 times in 18 different models of glider, and some of his longer flights reached nearly a quarter of a mile. Then, on a windy summer day in 1896, Otto made his final flight. While testing a new method of steering, he was caught by a gust of wind which caused his craft to stall, tip over and crash. The next day, Otto, 49, died of a fractured spine. His last words to his weeping brother were, "Sacrifices must be made."

In 1903, at Kitty Hawk, North Carolina, the Wright Brothers effectively put hang gliding on hold for more than half a century with their successful 12-second flight in a 13-horsepower machine, the "Flyer." It was the first time in history that a machine carrying a man had raised itself into the air by its own power, had flown without reduction of speed, and had landed at a point as high as that from which it had started.

Hang gliding in its modern form began in 1951 with the invention of a stable, predictable airfoil in the shape of an arrowhead by Francis M. Rogallo, a NASA engineer. The modern Rogallo consists of a framework of aluminum tubing with a Dacron sail stretched over it so that when the wind catches it, it billows out—thwock!—in a manner suggestive of a huge bird's wing during a glide. This billowing sail becomes, in aerodynamic terms, an airfoil. Stainless steel guy wires stretch from various points on the wings to the control bar. The control bar, which is beneath the wings at the glider's center of gravity, is one-inch aluminum tubing in the shape of a large isosceles triangle that the pilot grasps while flying. The two equal sides of the triangle measure six feet, while the base is five feet long. By shifting his body while grasping the control bar, the pilot is able to steer the glider.

Though the Rogallo has been around since 1951, it was not until the mid-Seventies that significant numbers of people began to take up hang gliding. In 1973, when hang gliding was still very much a fringe sport, Rudy Kishazy flew from Mt. Blanc, the tallest mountain in Europe, setting both altitude and distance records and capturing the attention of an international community of adventurers. The sport caught on in the U.S., threatening to become a full-blown national craze. Its appeal was obvious, and for many, irresistible. Because the Rogallo allows accomplished pilots the freedom and mobility to do whip stalls, chandelles, spiral dives, 360-degree turns, lazy-eight turns and hammerhead stalls, hang gliding conformed more closely than technologically advanced aircraft to the ancient dream of avian flight.

The downside was that the increased popularity of the sport brought with it a concomitant rise in fatalities:

1971	3
1972	10
1073	50
1978	86

(In 1978, when hang-gliding deaths were at their peak, Metropolitan Life issued figures showing that there were between 20,000 and 60,000 hang-glider pilots in the U.S. If the lower figure were used, they pointed out, then hang gliding was the third most dangerous sport, behind only flying home-made aircraft and skydiving. If the higher figure were used, it ranked sixth behind, additionally, mountain climbing, flying super-lights and scuba diving. In either case, the public's image of hang-glider pilots had now deteriorated to something resembling recreational Kamikazee pilots.)

Negative publicity cooled the ardor of all but the most dedicated, and many pilots traded in their gliders for running shoes. Not, however, Case and Sterios. By 1973 pretty, hip 23-year-old Jan Case was both an accomplished pilot and an innovative teacher. She was, as far as she knows, the first to apply kinesthetic teaching methods to hang gliding. "First thing, I'd have two or three students set up each glider. That gets them working as a team, takes their mind off the upcoming flight and gives them confidence in their equipment."

It was, in fact, lack of confidence in the equipment Chandelle was putting out that prompted Case and Sterios to leave Denver. They arrived back in San Francisco in their loaded V.W. van, hang glider and gear lashed to the top, the name "CHANDELLE SKY SAILS" still painted on the side, looking like refugees from some Sixties novel. They were quickly assimilated into the hang-gliding community, whose "home airport" was a series of cliffs south of Fort Funston called Westlake, where steady ocean breezes strike the hills and deflect upward, creating a favorable "ridge lift."

Case and Sterios found they could support their hang-gliding habit by selling gliders and equipment from their home. In addition, Case padded the beaches of Northern California giving hang-gliding lessons, five bucks per, no reservations needed. Working 5-6 days a week, she began to develop a critical eye for what made people excel.

"Hang gliding is 90% mental, 10 physical," she asserts in her naturally ebullient tone. "It takes very little physical coordination. Anyone who's reasonably healthy can learn to fly. You can tell who the novice pilots are because they're in shape from hiking up the hills. Advanced pilots fly from mountains that are too high to hike, that require cars to get to the top. So they're the ones with the beer bellies. . . .

"Hang gliding is a perception sport, an intuitive sport, a finesse sport. Understanding how the glider works is essential. Gymnasts tend to make good pilots; football players don't. I remember giving lessons to a husband and wife. He was a big, strong ex-football player who battled the glider with a death grip; his wife, a dancer, was very tuned into the sport. She had a good feel for the currents and the craft. She soared and he dropped like a stone. . . .

"You need a certain amount of psychological stability and control up there. Flying is no place to try to prove something to someone else. High-strung people should wait to fly when they're calm. . . ."

Case has been involved with the sport long enough to see enormous changes. In the early Seventies, she says, early pilots lacked the ethereal grace they display today. "It was basically a fly-from-top-get-to-bottom type of experience. The gliders weren't very responsive to weight shifts. I remember at the 1973 Lilienthal meet, the male pilots were flailing all over the place. Changing directions was a huge task. But then Donnita Hall came flying in, looking so pretty. She kept her feet together and made a smooth touch-down landing . . . that's when it all clicked for me. She was doing it the way it was meant to be done. Women were meant to fly!

"I went over to her and she let me lift her glider, which weighed 27 pounds, and I thought, 'Wow, fantastic, I can lift it!'"

Hall left Case with three enduring lessons:

1. Make them build a glider you can carry.
2. Don't try to stay up with the men or you'll get hurt ("and she was a lot tougher than I am").
3. Do it for fun ("as opposed to ego, conformity, machismo").

"Do it for fun—that was what Sterios had told me, too. It's the key to why I'm still in the sport."

Case has taken a personal interest over the years in helping women fly. "I've seen so many girls who have come out to the site and said, 'Oh, I'd love to do that.' But then they stop themselves with all the made-up reasons why not: 'I'd never have the guts, it's too expensive, I haven't the time. . . .' Then they'd watch me do it and a lot of those reasons would evaporate. They'd realize there aren't any physical limitations. I don't exactly come across as a brute, my hair in pigtails, looking about thirteen years old. I'd hear things like, 'Oh, mommy, that little kid's doing it. Can't I do it too?'"

Jan believes that hang gliding is its most dangerous right after a pilot has passed the beginner stage. "After six months or a year," she says, "there occurs what we call the Intermediate Syndrome. That's when a pilot has gotten through the beginning stage without breaking his glider, or his bones, and he starts hearing little voices inside his head saying, 'Well, shoot, there really aren't many risks.' We used to hold our breath when we saw students get to that intermediate yahoo stage. It's like the sailor who says, 'What? Small craft warnings—No problem, I'm hot.'"

Case remembers her own brush with Intermediate Syndrome: "I thought I was invincible," she says. "I had it made! It was so easy to soar and I could even land now. Then one day I got blown into barbed wire by a big gust of wind and almost killed—all because I wasn't paying attention. I was lucky enough to survive, which made me start taking it seriously again."

Case also believes strongly in Advanced Syndrome. "New problems await a pilot who has flown for a few years," she says. "Now he's a Hang IV and a hotshot in the community. People know his name and look up to him. Once again he starts thinking he's invincible, so he zips off to a 3,000-foot hill and gets a quick 8,000-foot vertical gain. He doesn't have his warm clothes on, but who cares?—he's invincible! He starts doing aerobatics, thinking, 'I've been up and down the normal way at least a thousand times, so let's see if I can do this upside down. . . .'

"My own formula for staying alive involves never crossing two unknowns. A new site and a new piece of equipment—that's two unknowns—or being tired and a new site, or being tired and a new piece of equipment. If there are two unknowns, two shaky things, then I won't fly. That's my rule, but sometimes it's really hard. . . ."

Like the first time she went to Big Sur, which is to pilots what the Potomac is to paddlers. "It truly is a mystical place to fly," Jan says, "and I was really looking forward to it. But as I started unloading the car I realized I had a brand-new harness that I'd never flown with before. New place, new equipment—two unknowns. I almost cried, I wanted to fly so bad. But I didn't do it; instead we continued south to Guadalupe sand dunes, where I blew two takeoffs in a row because I wasn't used to the new harness."

In 1974, a novice pilot was killed at Funston, the first ever Bay Area hang-gliding fatality. It precipitated the inevitable bad press and cries for regulating the sport. Case was selected to represent the hang-gliding community to the city council. She argued persuasively that the Fellow Feathers, as the local pilots called themselves, should have control over the area so that they—the real experts—could make sure that only qualified pilots flew there. She presented them with a draft of what she asserted would be a good regulatory plan. To her surprise, they agreed to the plan.

"The city council gave us a six-month trial period," she explains. "We put in a rating system that predated the one eventually used by the United States Hang Gliding Association. To fly there, you had to have at least a Hang III and 10 hours of soaring. After a pilot put in his 10 hours of air time, he had to get 3 sponsors—people who were already Westlake pilots to sign their name to his card. For pilots traveling through, we required a Hang IV, soaring experience, and the sponsor had to be with him at all times. If someone screwed up, his sponsors got burned; so nobody screwed up."

At Funston, the club rules were eventually adopted as park policy. If need be, park rangers could ticket defiant pilots, but for the most part it was still left to the pilots to police the site. "We all monitored," says Case. "At our club meetings we'd talk about how to handle the guy who says, 'The hell with you, I'm going to fly anyway.' We agreed that we would take diplomacy as far as we could, but that if that didn't work, we'd get five other members and move the guy's kite back from the take-off area. We started a rumor early on that we were carrying wire cutters. Then we put out the word that if anyone had to cut a set of wires to keep someone from flying that we would replace them free of charge. We never had to cut any wires, but the word was out that you just didn't screw up in the San Francisco area or you'd get your wires cut.

"All that was necessary because of the ego that finds its way to the top of a mountain. A guy might be scared to death, but he probably won't admit it to anyone. I've seen pilots who supposedly had loads of experience end up in the water. I've had guys come up to me and tell me they had a Hang V rating (like hitting a "five-bagger" in baseball). Another giveaway is if they have trouble putting their wing together. Or they get blown over in the set-up area."

San Francisco was only the beginning of Case's political career. Over the next few years, she spearheaded drives to legalize hang gliding in national forests, parks and wilderness. She launched a letter-writing campaign, sending "If-You-Care" letters to thousands of people, to anyone who knew anything about hang gliding. She also made presentations to civic groups, pointing out, ad nauseum, that "hikers have an impact on the wilderness that we seem to be able to live with, yet a pilot's impact is only half that of a hiker—we only walk up the hill."

As a result of her labor, places like Mt. Tamalpais and Yosemite National Park were opened up to hang gliding.

In 1975 Case and Sterios split up. "We were in the middle of making love one night," she remembers, "when we started talking about whether or not a glider had been shipped the day before. We decided the business had become the best part of our relationship."

The following year, Sterios was at Funston when a friend came in for a landing, then walked over to him and said, "My glider isn't flying right. Would you try it for me?" It was not an unusual request, for by then Lee had solidified his reputation as the "old man of the mountain."

"Sure," he said, "what's it doing?"

"When I speed up, it feels like it wants to turn upside down. Would you take it out over the water?"

Sterios launched the glider and flew out over the blue Pacific waters, man and wing momentarily silhouetted against the setting sun. Dipping his wing, he eased through a 180-degree turn and headed back toward the beach. As he pulled in on the control bar, the glider suddenly tucked, one wing broke, and Lee and the glider smashed into the wet sand at tide line.

The telephone message reached Jan at the shop: "Lee has gone in," a voice said in the vernacular. Case raced to his side and was with him several hours later when he died of a cerebral hemorrhage. "Being with him in those last hours," she says, "I could feel him communicating to me that everything was okay. It wasn't scary; there was no desperation. After all, he died doing what he loved to do . . . and doing it for someone else."

In the Eighties, technical advances in the manufacture of gliders have made them "pitch positive," meaning that when the pilot has the craft nose-down and takes his hand off the control bar, the glider will right itself. The result has been a plummeting death rate. "They're designed to fly now," Jan says with no trace of bitterness. "In the beginning they were really nothing more than directional parachutes."

Today, good pilots with good equipment have the instinct and the intuition necessary to utilize those invisible cells of air called thermals. Created when the ground has been heated by the sun, thermals can best be compared to immense bubbles of rising air. They are to the hang glider pilot what water current is to the canoeist.

Case usually tries to stay near the core of the thermal, letting it carry her higher and higher, her altimeter beeping faster and faster. When the thermal begins to dissipate, she will fly over to another one. "Thermal flying is state-of-the-art technique," she says. "The difference between intermediate and advanced pilots is the ability, the intuition, necessary to find thermals and prolong the flight. Thermal flying is the most gratifying—you found it, you earned it!"

Case herself favors big circular thermals because, she says, "I'm a lazy flyer. I fly because it feels good. I've probably done a thousand flights, counting training and demonstrations, and 750 of them have been for pure pleasure."

Today, pilots have climbed to more than 10,000 feet above their takeoff point and flown hundreds of miles without touching down. Such radical advances have made a travesty of distance events in big-time hang-gliding competitions. "If you're into cross-country flights these days," says Case, "you need chase crews and two-way radios—and lots of time. We've gotten away from longevity records because world-class pilots will stay up all day. It usually comes down to who can take the most drugs, which is something we try not to encourage."

As for the "Best and Beautiful Places to Fly," Case says, "The legendary spots are Big Sur, Yosemite, Nepal, Hawaii, even Mt. Tamalpais. For rowdy mountain flying, it's hard to beat Telluride, Colorado. But 'best' is very subjective, depending largely on the ability of the pilot. The first question you have to ask is, 'Are you a beginner?' If so, then ideal conditions mean smooth hills, smooth winds—about 5-7 mph—blowing uphill at just the right angle...."

FORT FUNSTON, MAY, 1988: On this day, flying conditions are not ideal—even for an advanced pilot like Case. The winds—gusting, swirling—are marginal at best. She is there to fly, but at this moment considers it a dicey proposition. A few pilots have launched, but many more have not. The coastal ridges are dotted with clusters of pilots next to colorful wings that resemble huge, somnolent moths. Thus far, Case is content to sit near her own glider and admire the undulating coastline and the pale-blue Pacific waters.

At 38, she is still tiny, pretty and appears younger than her years. Because she weighs less than the men, she must follow a different set of rules. Though she is able to launch in less wind and soar in less lift, she lacks the strength and weight to cope with winds suitable for a 200-pound man. She will wait.

She reflects on the sensuous high that ridge soaring offers— "just me and the wind in the wires"—and that thought tempts her to fly. She has, in fact, launched in such winds before, but today she doubts she will risk it. Why such a change of heart? Perhaps it's the influence of her friend Eric who, at the age of 74, recently came to her for hang-gliding lessons. Eric had certainly affected her outlook—before him she would have launched on a day like today. But Eric was hang gliding at 74, and when she was 74 she was going to be hang gliding, too. So even if she didn't fly today, or tomorrow, or for the rest of this year, she had her whole life to fly. And the sport was only getting better. The equipment, the experience—everything was getting better. So what was the hurry?

Rick Sylvester in final preparation for "For Your Eyes Only"

THE MISADVENTURER

"Giving up is the ultimate tragedy."
—Robert J. Donovan

Rick Sylvester stood on the rim of El Capitan, looking out over Yosemite Valley and pondering his fate. Far below, 3200 feet below, lay a brown winter meadow. Sylvester stared at that meadow with particular interest, for it was to be his landing target. Nine-hundred feet from the base of El Capitan, beyond a grove of pine trees. A realistic goal, he thought, but watch out for those trees. He tried to recall that quickie last-minute lecture on tree-landing procedures, something about trying to hook the chute over the top of the tree, something about covering the chin and groin areas ... ah hell, he'd make the meadow. He had nothing if not spirit.

He ski-stamped the snow for the hundredth time, smoothing imaginary blemishes on the run. It was cosmetic surgery, for the run had been laboriously packed and sculpted into the wee hours by himself and his support crew. Most people imagined the top of El Capitan to be smooth and flat, but it was far from that. The gullied granite, littered with bushes and branches, offered no natural ski run. It had taken many man-hours to provide that. The Jump simply wouldn't have been possible without the aid and comfort of friends and crew. Load-bearers, ski-run packers, camera people—most doing more than one job— he hoped he wouldn't disappoint them all by dying. He wondered, Who is the patron saint of parachute-skiing? Or should it be ski-parachuting?

Paraskiing? Oh, what did it matter? It didn't figure to be as mainstream a sport as baseball . . . or even midget wrestling. It was in fact virgin sport—until now.

It had come to him during a sleepless night. A preposterous idea: Be the first to ski off El Capitan, the largest monolithic piece of granite in the world. Two months later he added the parachute, creating a realistic stunt—at least in his eyes. To the others who didn't see it that way and asked "Why?" he replied, "Because I thought of it."

Obstacles arose, the first and most glaring of which was that Sylvester had never sky dived in his life. "However," he says, "it had always been on my list of things to learn."

He learned. Two weeks of lessons at the Antioch airport (scheduled for three, one week was "fogged" out), during which he made an incredible 53 jumps. "It was really a crash course," he says, "no pun intended. Stepping out of a plane at 2800 feet has to be the most unnatural thing in the world. I won't even try to describe that first jump, but just imagine all your moments of truth multiplied together."

Near the end of the training, Sylvester began to practice maneuvers that might be specifically applicable to El Capitan. He attached to his feet blocks of wood—two by fours—with ski bindings mounted on them to simulate the ski release. He intentionally left the plane as awkwardly as possible, upside down, tumbling, spinning, to see how quickly he could right himself. As he explains, "Who knew in what position I'd find myself flopping over the side of El Cap?"

"When you talk about adventure," Sylvester continues, expounding on a topic close to his heart, "one of the concomitants has to be 'the unknown'. And there were a lot of unknowns with the Jump: What about the updrafts? Would I get away from the wall? And after I chucked the skis, what would happen to them?

"My original idea had been to jump and immediately open the chute. But after talking to an acquaintance who jumped out of a plane with skis on—'a nightmare of balance,' he called it—I abandoned that idea. After all, one of the main functions of the jumpsuit is to cover any protrusions which could conceivably catch on the deploying canopy, and what greater protrusion than a pair of 215-centimeter skis?"

Balancing his skis on his shoulder, Sylvester began a slow trudge towards the top of the ski run looking like a condemned man taking his last walk. Although neither a highly religious nor superstitious man, he found himself ruminating on the miraculous. A Russian lieutenant fell 22,000 feet and lived....A Yugoslavian stewardess dropped 31,000 feet in the tail section of an exploded airliner and made it....If the chute doesn't open, will I make it? Will I be in that elite group? That one in a million? Just then a tiny voice spoke up: "Don't count on it."

He thought of the two guys who had leaped from the top of El Cap with parachutes on their backs. Failing to get away from the wall, they banged against it all the way down, badly bruising themselves, leaving one with a permanent limp when he landed hard in the scree field at El Cap's base. But hell, they'd broad-jumped it, plus they'd ignored the prevailing advice and jumped in the afternoon when the updrafts were unfavorable. He would get away from the wall....

In parachute school, he practiced "tracking," a body position in free fall in which the arms are held next to the sides, as in ski jumping. In tracking, also known as Delta position, the jumper accelerates from 120 to 160 miles per hour, all the while adding horizontal distance to his vertical descent. And to reach that meadow, Sylvester needed at least 900 feet of horizontal distance.

He thought of Miura—"The Man Who Skied Down Everest," and the only other skier Sylvester knew of who ever employed a parachute. (Actually there was another, but Sylvester was mercifully unaware of him. Some European had skied off a Dolomite cliff and died landing on a ledge 600 feet down before he could pull his rip cord.) Sylvester decided that his stunt was scarier than Miura's. He had skied down a lot of mountains, including most of Mt. McKinley, and had always felt that he was still a part of the earth. And when he jumped out of a plane, he had already divorced himself from the earth. But coming down the ski run, he would be very much a part of it, with no real sense of the terrible abyss, then suddenly—!

There were other problems, too. He had the Jump divided into three phases:

1. The Ski—700 feet of slightly inclined ski-packed snow. Here he might fall and lose speed and not get away from the wall, or separate a shoulder and not be able to pull the rip cord. True, he'd

skied for years—both downhill and cross country—but seldom with a 40-pound parachute on his back. "With that load, I couldn't ski well in the egg or tuck position," he says. "On the one hand, I figured the faster I skied the further from the wall I'd get. But that also increased my chances of falling and dribbling over the side. As with all things in life, it'd be a compromise."

2. The Fall—3200 feet, about half of it free fall as it turned out. Once away from the wall, he had to chuck the skis (where would they go?) and open the chute at the proper time. A mistake anywhere could mean disaster.

3. The Landing—ideally in the meadow. If not . . . ?

There was little in Rick Sylvester's early background that augured a future in adventurism. After his birth in Brooklyn in 1942, his family moved to Southern California when he was three. His father was an attorney who, among his other pursuits, got into building tract homes after World War II. He happened to be building them in Anaheim about the time Disneyland went up, with the result that Mr. Sylvester made a considerable amount of money.

The three kids went to Beverly Hills High School, where they did minimal hobnobbing with the sons and daughters of the rich and famous. "Well, if you want them you always have a few names to toss around," says Sylvester. "Glenn Ford was my scoutmaster—a nice man. And I went to school with Danny Thomas's kids, and Groucho's daughter. Leo Durocher lived across the street. . . ."

Although Sylvester was an accomplished collegiate wrestler, most of his early plaudits were for intellectual achievements. An honor student, he was graduated from U.C. Berkeley in 1965 with a double major: Sociology and Scandanavian Literature and Language. Seeking to prolong his studies, he applied to the Institute for English Speaking Students in Stockholm. He was accepted and he and his wife Rhoda journeyed abroad.

"I'd always been a student," he explains. "I was reluctant to let academic life come to an end. But sitting in a sterile library pouring over books on Swedish Social Order, about the world's most boring subject, at least to me, while outside, ten feet in every direction, everything seemed new and exotic, I sensed the end of my academic career, such as it was."

Before he had left Berkeley, Rick had found a brochure for the

International School of Modern Mountaineering. It was founded
and operated by a world-famous climber, John Harlin, the "Blond
God", as he was known in climbing circles. During his time in
Stockholm, Sylvester exchanged a few letters with Harlin. "It was
mostly over a financial matter," he says. "The school was $100 a
week, which was a lot of money to me. I was living on about $1000 a
year—getting a little help from my family—but I knew I was going
to that climbing school. To seem less selfish, at least in my own eyes, I
signed my wife up too. But I had a gut feeling that she'd drop out
after the first day, and I wanted to find out if I'd get that other $100
back. But then Harlin was killed climbing on the North Face of the
Eiger—he fell 4000 feet when his rope broke—and the money didn't
seem so important. It was a sobering introduction. I thought, if this
can happen to one of the greatest climbers in the world, what's in
store for me?"

Rick and Rhoda arrived at the climbing school in Leysin,
Switzerland, which had been taken over by Harlin's climbing
partners, Dougal Haskin and Don Whilans, world-class climbers
themselves. As Rick predicted, his wife dropped out after the first day;
but he stayed on, even signing up for a second week when typically
bad alpine washed out several days of the first week-long course.

Now Rhoda began to get really annoyed. "She was not overly
adventurous," Sylvester says. "An athletic event for her was driving a
stick shift. She was anxious to get back out on the tourist trail, to get
on to Rome-Paris-London."

Ironically, it was Rhoda who helped Rick get his first big
climbing opportunity. He explains: "My wife came up to our room
near the end of that second week and said that Layton Kor (who had
been on the Eiger when Harlin was killed) was downstairs looking
for a climbing partner. She thought he meant for the day, but he
wanted to go to the Dolomites in Northern Italy for a week or so, and
he knew I had a car—that was a big deal. Climbers are always
looking for partners. My first four climbing partners were Don
Whillans, Dougal Haston, Yvon Chouinard and Layton Kor—four
of the best in the world. That's like going out to play baseball for the
first time with Pete Rose.

"So we gathered up Rhoda, and Layton's French girlfriend, and
the four of us set off for the Dolomites. I remember seeing a sign at
one point: VENICE—86 KILOMETERS. Oh, Rhoda's eyes lit up.

Venice! It is Mecca to the sightseer. But I was driving, and I guess right there I made the choice between my marriage and climbing. We did not go to Venice."

Climbing with Layton Kor, Sylvester was not an immediate popular success. "It was a true baptism by fire," he says. "I couldn't do the first pitch, couldn't even get off the ground doing the first moves of the first pitch of the first climb we tried. For six days he dragged me up some tough climbs, always leading, always keeping the rope taut, which was no fun. But on the last day, doing our hardest route, I could feel I was getting it a bit. I wanted to yell to him to slack up on the rope and let me climb. . . ." After a reflective pause, Sylvester adds, "Even though in the beginning I was nearly catatonic with fear, deep down I knew the climbing life was for me."

At the end of that week, Rick rendezvoused with a fellow ISMM student and he and Rick drove off to find the Matterhorn. "Now, as a technical climb, many of the Matterhorn routes are not that difficult," Sylvester explains. "Story has it that a four-year-old girl and a ninety-year-old man have done it, and four Swiss guides tried to push a cow to the top. But a lot of climbers have been killed on the Matterhorn and we were still novice climbers. Timing was critical: We had to get started at first light, which we didn't do; then my partner lagged behind, until finally he said he was turning back. I kept on, and suddenly realized that I was soloing the Matterhorn! With my late start, the guides coming down the mountain were all screaming at me to turn around. One tried to physically restrain me. But I made it to the top and most of the way back down before darkness forced me to bivouac on the mountain. No sleeping bag. And one of those near-freezing alpine nights that made sleep impossible. But the next day when I returned to Leysin where my wife was staying, I was elated. I burst in on her, screaming, 'I climbed the Matterhorn! I soloed the Matterhorn!' "

" 'I'm leaving you,' she said."

Sylvester's boots crunched rhythmically in the snow as he moved to the top of the ski run. He stopped and watched a raven for a moment, admiring its silent, effortless flight. Here and there members of his team chatted and worked. It was not as quiet as usual on the top of El Cap, he thought.

Suddenly the "why" leapt out at him. Why was he here? Why

wasn't he home reading about someone else doing it? The bird glided out of sight; the questions brought answers. The Jump was a logical extension of all that he'd done, he decided. He'd climbed the vertical walls of the rock four times, spent close to a month's time dangling from its sides. Here was a chance to reverse it and be much quicker about it. He continued walking, remembering that thought-provoking graffiti: "A person can live intensely only at the cost of one's soul."

Sylvester's journey from married student to single climber had dramatic impact. "Suddenly I was introduced to a new way of life," he says. "With its own special mountain bohemian subculture. I've never left it. As a result, my life has become qualitatively better. Instead of fifty weeks a year in the city and two in the mountains, I've reversed it."

He moved to Squaw Valley, where the skiing is good but the living isn't always easy. He answered an ad in *Summit* magazine: "Climbers Wanted for Ski Patrol in Alpine Meadows."

Sylvester, shaking his head, says, "It seemed like no one had ever wanted climbers for anything before, but this guy knew that compared to climbing, ski patrol work is trivial. He knew that climbers who could ski could do the job well. I only got $1.44 an hour, but I got to stay in the mountains."

He went to Yosemite and became part of that first wave of climbers who spent an entire season in the Valley. "Camp 4 was the climbers' campground," Sylvester says, dreamily. "Before I went to Yosemite, I had a view of climbers as the last romantic heroes. But living at Camp 4 was disillusioning. There was shoplifting from the village store. The higher-ups in the Curry Company and some of the rangers hated the climbers. When I first got there, my friends warned me not to wear my climbing boots to the store; it was a dead giveaway.

"So much of what I've done relates to that group of people I got involved with in Yosemite. It was one of those great periods—like Paris in the Twenties—only instead of it being artistic, it was an age of creative physical self-expression. It was always: Be the first, the highest, the furthest. Standards were pushed. The Jump was just a logical extension of it all."

For the next few years, Sylvester went on an adventure spree. Constantly improving, he made increasingly difficult climbs, including four different routes of El Capitan. During one memorable ten-day climb in which Rick led all the way, he and his partner ran out of food and water 2½ days before the top. In explanation, Sylvester is characteristically blasé. "We thought it would take five days," he says, shrugging. "They say you'll die in three days without water, but it's not true. In our case we were doing strenuous work and made it. It's one of those things: If you believe you'll die, then you may."

Over the years, Sylvester climbed many of the classic routes in the Alps, including the dreaded Eiger. He was one of six Americans invited by the Soviets to climb 24,590-foot Pik Communism in a mountaineering exchange program. He has climbed and skied down most of the major volcanoes in the western United States, and was the first American to ski down from the 20,320-foot summit of Alaska's Mt. McKinley—a run that dropped 14,000 feet and was about 20 miles long.

Not all of Sylvester's adventures proceed smoothly. One time he set off to ski the John Muir Trail, all 211 snow-covered, up-n-down miles of it, using—of all things—alpine skis. The primitive bindings made it rough going. As one of Sylvester's friends says, "The expedition was misplanned, but then, that's Rick. He has a way of turning an adventure into an epic—that's a borderline disaster in which everything turns out all right in the end." Starting near Mt. Whitney with a heavy pack, he soloed for 16 days and 140 miles. Says Sylvester, "I'm not as driven as some people might think. I'd stay in my sleeping bag until it warmed up, wouldn't get started till noon, then quit at dusk. In 16 days, the only sign of human life I saw were a few jets overhead." Finally, with the snow slushy, and the conversation stale, Sylvester exited with the usual misgivings about any failure. He neglected to inform his friends that he'd cashed in early, and while they fretted over his safety, he was recuperating in Squaw Valley. "It's all part of a misadventure label that follows me," he says. "For example, I've had more than one climbing partner touched by lightning...."

Another (mis)adventure was a climbing expedition to Patagonia, during which nearly everything that could go wrong did. "It was Murphy's Law," Sylvester says. "First of all, there were physical obstacles. We went to climb three towers, one of which had never been summitted. Patagonia has some of the worst weather in the world. The world's only major ice cap that isn't attached to either the Arctic or Antarctic is the Hielo Continental. Fierce winds move across the Pacific, pick up moisture and cold from the Hielo Continental, and first strike the Patagonia Towers. We spent two days securing fixed ropes, then two weeks in base camp sitting out storms. There were also the inevitable problems associated with having so many topnotch climbers, so many potential leaders, on one expedition. Too many stars make for bad climbing chemistry. We also had injuries. One of my partners crashed through a snow bridge and fell 40 feet into a crevasse with converging walls. He was wedged there with the only available rope in his pack down there with him. We finally retrieved him, but the thawing out was unbelievably painful. On that trip I had my first close contact with death: Two Argentinians who were on the mountain with us went off for an overnight climb and never came back. We searched and found their tent, battered down by the wind, rain and blowing snow. Its disheveled appearance has always loomed in my mind as a symbol of their fate.

"Finally, after three months of tying a few ropes and reading lots of books, we gave up and came home."

Sylvester reached the top of the ski run and began to collect himself. He was glad that he wasn't starting from the topmost point of El Cap, a low-angled granite dome a few hundred feet further back. He'd rejected the dome as a potential starting point when a crew member calculated that he'd be skiing at about 90 mph when he reached the edge. He'd leave that sort of thing to Steve McKinney.

When he picked up his helmet, some of the airmail stickers he'd plastered on it came loose and blew off in the wind. Insufficient saliva to wet the glue. Yes, he was a little nervous. He drank from a water bottle and reflected on how far they'd come. . . .

The Jump had originally been scheduled for the previous March. With the film crew on standby, Sylvester set off to assess snow conditions. Bearing a heavy load, he hiked, skied and snowshoed cross country to the top of El Cap, only to discover—no snow the last 1000 feet to the edge. "It was a shoveling job beyond practicality," he says. "At the time I wasn't sure I'd do it again. I figured my passion might cool."

But his passion persisted and the Jump was rescheduled for January. Rick and his support crew hauled themselves and their gear to the top, this time finding sufficient snow. They set about shoveling the snow, shaping it into a ramp to launch him over the last few feet of exposed exfoliating granite. They packed down a moderately-angled run, 1½ ski lengths wide and about 700-feet long. Except, to Sylvester standing at the top of it, it appeared exaggeratedly long and narrow. Like a long thread . . . unraveling?

Again we've had Murphy's Law, Sylvester thought. An aborted mission, personality clashes, equipment problems, communication hangups, weather worries and the pressure of time. But we're here. And ready. That is, everyone else appears ready. Time to ready Rick Sylvester. . . .

Suddenly the helicopter fired up and took to the air. A deafening whap-whap-whap that made him wince. Then panic. "I'm not ready yet," he cried into the din. "It's too early. I'm not prepared."

Sylvester checked his bindings; then the cords running beneath his pant legs that would release his skis (where would they go?). He checked and secured his boots, skis, helmet, gloves and poles, but the damn helicopter made it hard to concentrate and he worried that he was forgetting something. Fully geared, he stood at the top of the run with racing heart and mind. He went over every possibility: What about updrafts? What if he slipped and dribbled over the side? Or left a yellow trail of snow behind? Didn't pop the chute in time? Or knocked himself out? Or blacked out? The chute didn't open? He didn't make the meadow?

Then an old worry reared up again. There's a line in Yosemite National Park's regulations that says, "It is illegal to deliver an object by parachute from the rim to the valley floor." The legal question was: "Is a human an object?" The practical question was: "Will there be fifty rangers waiting on the valley floor to collect the evidence?" He and the crew had maintained a low profile, but that damn helicopter was enough to wake the dead.

Finally Sylvester ran out of delays. He quickly downed a half-bottle of beer, a small toast to the adventure, then adjusted his goggles, took a deep breath and signalled that he was ready. His crew signalled back. As he pushed off with a couple of skating steps, he wondered, was that really the signal? Maybe the cameras weren't ready. No, he must put that away. The film must rank behind the adventure. It's time to think about survival. . . .

With a chattering of skis, Sylvester roared down the run. He reached the lip (estimated speed 50-60 mph), dropped his poles and soared out into space on the ultimate ski jump. He easily cleared the wall, but at too steep an upward angle. Suddenly he was spun around like a child's pinwheel. Five quick somersaults dizzied him. Desperately, he tried to rally his senses....

Pull the cords, release the skis—they're off! Get stable, stomach to the earth, arch the back. Now tracking to get distance away from the wall, hands next to the sides. Christ! There's El Cap Towers, halfway down, maybe eight more seconds to earth! Pull! A soft jerk and the plummet becomes a glide. Whew! The valley floor stops rushing to meet him. Or he it. But now the meadow looks too far off. Where to land? An 80-foot pine tree looks wrong but inevitable ... snagged! Hung up amidst tangled chute cords and brittle branches. Too far to jump, but the tree is slender and a bearhug gets him to the ground with only a small scratch on the finger.

Today, Rick Sylvester lives in a moderately sized mountain home in Squaw Valley with his second wife, Betsy, and their two children. The general decor is of a Sesame Street motif—children's toys and drawings, coloring books—but there is an adult flavor to the abundant clutter, too. Dishes piled high in the sink, stacks of newspapers and books ("Who has time?"), magazines ("We subscribe to a dozen and a half—it can get out of hand.") and records ("Neither the TV nor the record player gets used too much."). Above the staircase is a poster-size blowup of the Jump, with Sylvester in mid-tumble. Under the garage is Rick's "shop," which is filled with dozens of pairs of skis, a jumble of climbing equipment, books, magazine clippings set out on the floor in a unique, open-air filing system, and bags of old newspapers that Sylvester "hasn't gotten to yet."

Rick is 45, but looks ten years younger. At 5' 6½" and 135 pounds, he is wiry, with taut, well-developed muscles and a healthy rawboned look. His curly, disheveled hair rarely feels a comb. With high cheekbones, his face seems to have been chiseled from rock. Perhaps it is life imitating art. "It's the nature of the climbing endeavor," Sylvester says. "The hard rock and ice wear away the outer layers until the kernel is exposed."

Although Rick Sylvester is a very good athlete and a hard-charging adventurer, he is also a cerebral man. He has written several magazine articles and reads voraciously. Possessing a graceful command of the English language, he is often asked to speak before audiences. His natural conversation has a wide sweep, but he evokes the most passion when he speaks of adventure:

"The British were the first to view mountains as sport. Primitive cultures looked upon mountains as fearful. Most wouldn't go near them. . . .

"Hemingway said that the three most dangerous sports are bull fighting, motor racing and mountain climbing. Today they might be free soloing, extreme skiing and kayaking. John Bachar is the American legend in free soloing. If athletes were paid on the basis of performance, Bachar would be among the highest paid. What he does is both awesomely dangerous and difficult. He solos things without a rope that most climbers can't do with a rope. His climbing has forced the creation of a new rating system: Class 1: you break every bone in your body; Class 2: brain death; Class 3: total death. . . .

"There are two ways to do things. You can be the best. Or you can go in the back door and be the first—like George Willig who climbed the World Trade Center. George is far from the best climber in the U.S., but with that feat he got a vast amount of media attention. . . .

"I haven't lifted weights since college, but I'm doing it now in a P.E. class. I realized that I was already near my peak in climbing unless I could add strength. Of course, no matter how much I work out, there will always be guys who are genetically stronger even if they don't work out at all. . . ."

On this day, Sylvester has cross-country ski raced, run five miles, and talked up a storm, yet he is in no mood to sit. He grabs a snow shovel and heads for the driveway. Shoveling a little, leaning a little, he speaks of the travail of filming the Jump. It seems that his camera crew atop El Cap, who was entrusted with the responsibility of capturing the event, were too afraid to stand near the edge even though they were roped in. Thus, as soon as Sylvester dropped below the lip of El Cap, he disappeared from camera range.

Two weeks later, he jumped again. This time he made the meadow—a stand-up landing—and got some good footage, but the chief ranger reacted coldly to the second jump, regarding it as a personal affront.

Imagine his reaction when, a year later, Sylvester jumped again. "I realized I still didn't have that perfect camera angle," he explains.

"I figured it would be from a helicopter hovering away from the rock, at an angle."

He wanted to make a comedy with the Jump as the conclusion. Part of this involved filming a fake fight scene atop El Cap, using the same camera crew and his friends dressed as rangers. In the excitement, he lost track of the time and didn't go off until late in the afternoon, when the updrafts had picked up. When he flew over the edge and released his skis, he was surprised when one of them landed on the open canopy, rested there a moment, then slid off. He realized that he was going to overshoot the meadow, so he performed the skydiver's standard maneuver of zigzagging back and forth to use up distance. By mistake, his chute touched the tip of a branch of a tall tree on the meadow's edge. The chute collapsed and Sylvester fell helplessly about 100 feet through branches that struck him like super karate chops. Against all odds, the chute got hung up on one of the last branches, about 50 feet above the valley floor, the last 40 feet being branchless trunk and much too wide to bearhug down. His support crew rescued him and he hustled out of the Valley. It all might have been worth it if the film had come out. But his camera crew on the valley floor had been forced to shoot right into the sun for a complete whiteout, and the camera on the chopper had malfunctioned, too.

In his haste, Rick left behind an expensive pair of boots. Rumor reached him that there was a warrant out for his arrest and that Chief Ranger Morehead was holding the boots for ransom. All he wanted in return was a promise from Sylvester that he wouldn't jump again, that he'd made his last flight over the edge of El Cap. But Sylvester considered the price too high and didn't claim the boots.

Sylvester's career as a movie mogul developed slowly. He had the spirit, the idea (an accident-prone waif tries to win the hand of his love by performing many of the feats that Sylvester does in real life), but little money. He started Absurd Joie de Vivre Film Company, but was only occasionally able to pay a camera crew. He refused to seek financial backing for his film because "I lack the patience to knock on doors. Also, I need the independence," he says. "Artistic or otherwise."

But, as Rick discovered, there is more than one way to break into the movies. Enjoying a fleeting fame from the Jump, he was asked to perform a similar feat on Baffin Island for a Canadian Club Whiskey magazine ad. When bad weather forced the cancellation of the new stunt, the ad agency superimposed onto a Mt. Asgard background a shot of Rick going off El Cap, then suddenly pulled the ad when word leaked out. Before they did, however, film producer Cubby Broccoli saw it, liked it, and hired Sylvester to perform the opening stunt in his new James Bond movie, "The Spy Who Loved Me."

SCENE: James Bond, schussing furiously, with the bullets of a band of pursuing KGB men zinging all around him, hurtles himself off 3,300-foot Mt. Asgard, chucks his skis, free falls for a while, then pulls the ripcord and floats to safety beneath a Union Jack canopy....

The skiing close-ups were Roger Moore, but the fall guy was, of course, Rick Sylvester. For that feat, which lasted only 30 seconds in the movie, Sylvester was paid $30,000, at that time the most ever earned for a single stunt.

"Essentially, I spent it all on my movie," Sylvester says, leaning on his shovel. "I went from living on $1000 a year to spending $1000 a day on that project. Since I started filming, I plunged over $60,000 of my own money into "Daydream Drummer," which is the working title of the movie.

A few years later, Sylvester was offered a job on the Bond movie, "For Your Eyes Only." Anyone who regards movie-making as high glamour would be disillusioned by talking with Sylvester, who, when discussing the subject, comes as close as he ever does to complaining. "I spent 2½ months in Greece, working long days. And it was frustrating working with the movie people. The filming was delayed until late summer, the result being that we ran into fall rains, which made the rock slippery and unclimable, and thus unfilmable on many days. I had three jobs: First, I doubled for Roger Moore. He's 6′ 5″ and I'm 5′ 6½″, so even with a $700 wig I didn't look very much—at least bodily—like Roger Moore. That prevented closeups. Second, I coached Roger on what he'd need to know and have to do to get through the on-location climbing scenes involving him (and not me as a stunt double). Risk sports are not high on Roger's list of preferences. And so it went against his grain to some degree. Third, I was the film's technical advisor for the climbing sequences. This is where we battled. The movie people wanted cliff-hanging action, so as to get bodies into the most spectacular positions. That's understandable, because for them the climbing was subservient to the story line. But it bothered me when they cut out the best, most exciting bits of climbing footage. Or tried to do something technically incorrect. Not only is it not the truth, it's unnecessary. You're spending all this money, why not do it right? If you're good enough you can retain the drama and still keep things technically correct to satisfy that one climber who might be in the audience of one of a thousand screenings. When someone does an article on me, I tell them: 'Say I pick my nose in public, I don't care as long as you tell the truth.'"

Betsy and the kids come home; Rick puts away his shovel and accompanies them upstairs. Pointing to his three-year-old son, Terray (named after the classic French alpinist Lionel Terray), Rick says proudly, "He's been on skis since he was two. I think he's going to be great...." Meanwhile, he's a great kid, bright and charming, as is his older sister, Cheyenne. They and their mother seem like ballast, adding stability to Rick's life, lest it spin out of orbit.

Betsy begins to fix dinner, the kids go off to play and Rick settles in at the dining-room table, surrounded by papers and books. He speaks of still another facet of Rick Sylvester: The Runner. The man has completed a phenomenal 110 marathons in seven or so years of running. "I collect them," he says, "like some climbers collect peaks. I usually do one every three or four weeks. Yeah, I know what they say about only running 2–3 a year, but that's for the guys down around 2:10. I'm around three hours (it's worked out that 80% of my marathons have been sub-three hours), and it doesn't take me long to recover."

Sylvester leans back in his chair and assumes a pedagogical pose. "The theory now is that you have at most a couple of great marathons in you. Look at Salazar. And in the '84 Olympics, there were only five completed marathons among the medal winners...."

Sylvester is admittedly an inveterate list maker. "I love setting goals," he says, "but I love even more crossing them off my list. For years on one list I had three main running goals: (1) To break three hours in the Tahoe Marathon; (2) To break 2:40 in any marathon (personal best 2:47); (3) To win one. I got the last one—I won the Porterville Marathon a couple of years ago in 2:52. After a second and a couple of thirds, it occurred to me that I could actually win one. And I did."

One time, suffused with ambition, Sylvester listed the goal of running every marathon in the world ... and each under three hours. "I was being totally unrealistic," he says with uncharacteristic dismissal. "First of all, they come and go, those races. The list is always changing. And some races are for women only." Sylvester's eyes light up in happy recollection. "Actually, I ran in one of those in San Francisco—women only. It was back when I still believed that all the marathons were possible, and I wanted to cross that one off my list. I finished it, but some of the women were less than overjoyed by my presence. I was threatened and almost beaten up by some male race monitors."

Rick Sylvester is so steady, so unwavering, that once again there is the suggestion of the climbing rock. He has quit on only four of his 110 marathons. "I don't like to quit," he says, "because then I can't cross it off my list."

Even in his marathoning, an element of misadventure sometimes exists. One weekend, Sylvester drove the six hours from Squaw Valley to Salinas for a marathon, arriving minutes after the race had started. The Salinas Marathon did not get crossed off his list.

In constant physical and intellectual motion, Sylvester packs more adventure into two days than most people do in a lifetime. In one weekend, he ran the Avenue of the Giants marathon in less than three hours, drove most of the night to begin carrying skis up 11,100-foot Mt. Lassen before dawn, summitted the peak, skied down the 4,000-vertical-foot descent of Lassen's North Face, then the next day ran the course for the double Dipsea race, before arriving back at his Squaw Valley home Sunday night.

"That was before fatherhood," Sylvester says, "maybe even marriagehood. Being the father of two is an adventure in itself. I'm disorganized but basically responsible. I'm not willing to go away for months at a time anymore. I don't want to be away from my kids that long."

That's not to say, at age 45, that Rick Sylvester's life of adventure is over. Merely transmuted. A few months after this conversation, Sylvester and his family were scheduled to go to Europe. The focal point? "The Paris Marathon," he says with a slight octave change. "I'll do some climbing, too, but I'm looking forward to that marathon. It's an evening race and I'm an evening person. I'm also an incurable romantic. When I'm home reading about a race in, say, Chicago, it seems like the most romantic thing in the world. But when I get to the starting line, reality hits: it's just another hard, (more often than not) unaesthetic 26.2 miles that lie ahead. I say I'm incurable because I should know better by now—I've run 110 of those things."

And just what makes Rick run? And climb? And ski? "It all stems from an attitude," he explains. "If you believe Eric Erickson's theories on personality formation, it was probably engendered in me by the time I was three, although there sure wasn't any encouragement from my parents. I went against the grain there." Sylvester pauses, reflects, then says with remarkable candor, "Maybe the whole thing is nothing more than the small-man's complex run amuck. Maybe I'm just compensating for all those years of being the smallest kid in my gym classes."

It goes beyond that, of course, as Sylvester freely admits. "I guess I'm just an experience junkie. I'm afraid of missing something."

Ironically, it is just that feeling that he evokes in others. Talking with Sylvester makes one feel, well, inexperienced. On his list of things yet to do? "I'd like to do a Dewar's Profile," he says, smiling. "For a favorite book, I'd put down the Atlas. For a romantic, it's a passport to adventure. For most of us, this is the only planet we'll ever know. When I was young one of my ambitions was to be the first person to set foot on three—one wasn't enough!—planets."

And will Rick Sylvester jump again? That is, Jump again?

He smiles and shrugs, leaving the option open. "Well, I still don't have that perfect camera angle, do I?"

Racing in Ireland

PEDAL PUSHER

"It is not death that a man should fear, but he should fear never beginning to live."
                                                    —Marcus Aurelius

ENDURANCE

John Howard recalls exactly when and where the seeds of his competitive cycling career were first planted: "In the fifth grade in Springfield, Missouri where I grew up—I was the dodge-ball champ...." He is sitting at the dining room table in his Southern California home, looking lean and fit and tough. With his receding curls of dirty-blond flyaway hair, his coarse, weathered skin, he looks every bit as old as his 39 years. "...It was then I learned that I had not just athletic ability but also the will to win."

Howard's comfortable two-story townhouse, 25 miles north of San Diego, is a monument to a man with not only the will but the talent to win. It is the home of a bicycle magnate. The dining room walls are festooned with dozens of plaques and awards, most a result of first-place cycling finishes; the garage is a clutter of bicycles, perhaps a dozen, most of them expensive, state-of-the-art models that were designed by or for Howard himself; in the living room, on an exercise stand, sits "The Outlaw," a sleek black racing bike that is Howard's latest design achievement.

He goes to the bike and looks upon it fondly, like a painter regarding his chef d'oeuvre. "This is the culmination of some real technological achievements," he says proudly. "We're the first to

129

use a drop-head tube. See how it slopes down in front. . . ." Indeed, the front tire appears tiny, almost fragile. "A 27-inch tire in the rear, a 24-inch in the front," he points out. "Air resistance is the single most detrimental thing in cycling; eliminate air resistance and you'll go faster."

Since he was a kid growing up in the Ozarks, John Howard has wanted to go faster, and further, than anybody. He received a bike in the first grade, but it was a clunker, a big heavy 3-gear Schwinn that was built for neither speed nor distance. When John and his brother were in junior high, they started their own business (landscaping in good weather, selling firewood in bad), then poured their first profits into a pair of the new ten-speed touring bikes that had hit the market.

Although Howard continued to run track—the mile—and play football and baseball, his love affair with the bicycle had begun. "Springfield in the Fifties was right out of a Norman Rockwell painting," he says. "In high school, riding my bicycle everywhere instead of driving a pickup truck got me branded a weirdo." He smiles. "I never minded that too much. I've always kind of thrived on it. I like playing the crazy."

It wasn't just Howard's peers who looked askance at his obsession with pedaling. His track coach ranted at him for . . . what else? . . . riding his bicycle. "Coach thought I was riding my bike too much, so he gave me a choice: biking or running the mile. I chose biking."

Then one day he quit football. Just walked off the field during practice, got on his bicycle and rode off, never to return. He was off the team and his father was angry. An ex-football player himself, he lived vicariously through John and his athletic endeavors. He wanted a football player, not a kid on a bike.

"Looking back," says John, "I realize that what he really wanted was success. When he saw that I was a success in bicycling, he became—and still is—my biggest fan."

Upon graduation from high school in 1966, Howard set his sights on the 1968 Olympics in Mexico City. He began to train hard, riding 400–500 miles a week, exploring the frontiers of his mental and physical capabilities. "I made cycling a total commitment," he says.

In his first competition—a 102-mile road race—he finished second. Commitment approached obsession.

During the summer of 1968 Howard left home and traveled to Southern California for the Olympic cycling qualifiers. In order to make the team, a rider had to finish in the top four in either of two 100-plus mile road races. In the first race, a young, inexperienced John Howard finished back in the pack, out of the glory. In the second race, a still-young but no-longer inexperienced Howard came from behind to finish second and make the team.

Two days later—still 20 years old—he won the U.S. Cycling Federation National Championship.

Thus began Howard's reign as America's number-one cyclist. For the next decade he dominated the sport as no American has before or since: participating in three Olympics; winning countless races, including seven National Championships; winning—as no other American has ever done—a gold medal in individual cycling at the Pan Am games.

In 1979 he was selected Competitive Cycling's Rider of the Decade. As the senior member and number-one rider on the U.S. Olympic Team, he was in top form. He seemed to have it all—but still he wasn't satisfied. There were the losses, of course, particularly the disappointing performances in the Olympics (as the team's top rider, he is quick to explain, he had to ride both the road race and the team trials and consequently was unable to concentrate fully on either); but it was more than that.

Then one day it struck him: It was the whole "team" thing all over again. As a kid, he'd rejected football and baseball because they were team sports, requiring the support and cooperation of others. He'd left all that to be on his own in the supposedly solitary sport of cycling; but as a member of the U.S. Olympic Team, he was still expected to be a team player.

It didn't come naturally. He recalled one time in particular, in the World Championships in England, when the U.S. team was composed of Howard, a second rider who was perhaps his equal, and two who were definitely slower. Although the American team started eight minutes ahead of the Russians, Howard knew they couldn't hold it. Eventually the two weaker riders began to lag and the American team steadily lost time to the Russians. But the team, drafting off each other, stayed together.

When the Russians went by in their snappy red uniforms, their chains singing in perfect harmony, it occurred to Howard that they were his equals. "Sure, I wanted the U.S. team to do well, but I also wanted to join that Russian team. With them I could've ridden at my full potential."

Howard's innate lack of esprit de corps did not go unnoticed. It was undoubtedly a factor when the U.S. cycling coach kicked him off the team. "I pointed out that I was his best rider, Howard shrugs, "and he told me he was going with a younger team."

So Howard was once again "off the team." His feelings were hurt, but he consoled himself with the words his father oft spoke: "Eventually you outgrow everything."

That was fine as far as it went. But what of the competitive urges that still seethed within him? His marriage had gone sour, which seemed to make him all the more fiery. A 9-to-5 job was unthinkable—he needed more ... damn it, he needed adventure! Clearly, it was going to take extraordinary mortar to fill the gaps of his life.

Then *Sports Illustrated* ran an article about a new sport: The Hawaiian Ironman Triathlon—a grueling combination of a 2.4-mile swim, a 110-mile bike ride and a 26.2-mile run. When Howard had finished reading the article, he was a triathlete.

"I just decided to do it," he says. "Without knowing anything about it, I was sure I could take an hour off the winning time."

To his weekly 400 miles of cycling, he added 60 to 80 miles of running. His training routine broadened into a holistic, multi-sport regimen that eventually included calisthenics, mountain biking, swimming, running, kayaking, weights, and backpacking. He began to study sports pyschology, physiology, yoga and deep breathing for pain control.

Three weeks after starting, he completed a respectable 3:10 marathon, but developed shin splints and stress fractures. So he turned to swimming, which had never been more than an occasional activity for him. "I put some time in the pool," he says, "but I didn't bother to get a coach. As a result, I was just flogging the water, reinforcing my bad form. I have never really connected with what it took to be a good swimmer."

Nevertheless, in the next five years Howard completed 30 triathlons, including the Hawaiian Ironman four times. He won it in '81 and finished in the top ten in '80 and '84. In '82, however, someone dumped thousands of tacks on the road and he went down during the bike phase with two flat tires.

Despite his triathlon victories and consistent top-10 finishes, Howard has remained, predominantly, a one-sport athlete. Because he is one of the great cyclists of the world and has the will of Hannibal, he has been able to compensate for what is usually a poor swim and a mediocre run. In the '84 Ironman, prototypically, Howard was 750th after the swim, and third only to Dave Scott and Mark Allen after the bike. Until recently, he has never lost the bike phase of a triathlon. He is, heart and soul, first and foremost, a bicyclist. A world-class pedal pusher.

And will he do another triathlon? "Probably not," he says. "I like the better balance my body has as a result of cross training . . . but at 39, how much better am I going to get? My best time in the Ironman would've put me 15th this year. I mean I want to develop my full potential, but if I have no chance to win, what's the point?"

Maybe this: Howard gained more notoriety by winning the Ironman than by all his years of toil as an Olympic cyclist. As a result, he became somewhat of a hot property in the eyes of the sponsors of ultra-endurance events. So he took himself and his credentials to Pepsi-Cola and told them that he believed he could: one, win the Race Across America; two, break the 24-hour record on a bike; three, break the land-speed record on a bike.

They believed him, and John Howard became the next Pepsi Challenger.

Financial backing in place, Howard took aim on goal number one. He and a few other elite cyclists established what would be known as the Race Aross America, 2900 miles by bicycle, Los Angeles to New York City, stop-at-your-own-risk.

Howard's second-place finish still rankles him. "My support crew was too soft on me," he is quick to say. "Instead of pushing me out of bed, they let me sleep in. I got about three hours of sleep a night." He shrugs. "It turned out to be too much."

Although he was nearly killed by a car in Pennsylvania, and suffered compression damage to the ulnar and medial nerves in his hands and arms that still bothers him today, Howard completed the coast-to-coast cycle in 10 days, 11 hours. "I was cooked for weeks after that," he says. "Of all the things I've ever done, the Race Across

America was definitely the toughest. For 10 days it was just biking and eating and biking and napping and biking. . . ."

Clearly, it's the biking that thrills him. And it's more than the competition. He's simply in love with the sport, as evidenced by his paean: "There's nothing like a bike race for drama. You can watch the strategies unfold, with all the variables of tactics, terrain and riders' strengths. It's like a chess game; sometimes you don't know who'll win until the final seconds. You can be the strongest rider and still lose because of tactics. You can't win on sheer 'horse power' alone. . . .

"There's something about covering a lot of ground under your own power. It has to do with the blue sky, the fresh air, the gears working perfectly. When things are just right, the bike is a physical extension of yourself. Ideally, there should be a synthesis of movement between bike and rider. This gives you an incredible high. And once you've found it, nothing else will do."

But surely competition must be at the core. Like most great athletes, Howard hates to lose; and finishing second in RAAM just made him all the more determined to win a guts-out endurance bike race. Pursuant to that, only a month after going coast-to-coast, he issued an open challenge to RAAM winner Lon Haldeman, and some other world-class cyclists, to meet him in Central Park for the 24-Hour Bike Race.

"None of them showed up," Howard says in bully tones, his mustache bristling. "They knew what they were in for—I was in great shape."

He lived up to his own pre-race hype by riding 475 miles, a new 24-hour record.

The following year he was back with still another extraordinary performance. "It rained that year," he remembers, "which floated the broken glass to the surface. I had seven flat tires. . . ."

And still outdid himself, riding 512 miles—(an average of 21.3 mph, a record that stood until the past spring, when Howard broke it again with a 519-mile ride in Clearwater, Fl.).

"No rest stops," he adds, with a supercilious smile. He has anticipated the question that is never far from the listener's lips: "I used an external catheter."

SPEED

BONNEVILLE SALT FLATS, JULY 1985: John Howard jammed his huge freckled hands into his leather gloves and squinted out at the shimmering salt beds. White heat wigwagged on the horizon. Utah in July: It was well over a hundred degrees, and Howard was hot and tired of waiting. For two days he'd been waiting. Now what was the delay? First they were a Go, then they weren't. If it weren't the bike, it was the car, or the wind, or the salt. He was reminded of the old Army expression: "Hurry up and wait."

He'd come to the Salt Flats to break the human-powered land speed record (in the summer, because that was the only time they could count on the salt being right), but for every four-minute run there was a delay of three or more hours. It was necessary, of course, he knew that. Meticulous cleaning of salt from the bike, cooling down and checking the race car—all necessary because it was his butt on the line. But he was not a patient person and he wished like hell they could just get on with it.

He removed his gloves and took a drink from the water bottle offered by an aide. It was hard to get enough fluids. Someone figured that he sweated away four to 5 pounds on every run. Part of the problem, of course, was that he was a tad overdressed for triple-digit temperatures. Colorfully garbed from head to toe in a custom-made yellow helmet, red and yellow motorcycle racing leathers, turquoise bootcovers, black cycling shoes, he looked good. Still, he reckoned, it was about the hottest he'd ever been.

At last, the Green Light! Howard's partner, professional driver Rick Vesco, fired up the race car, and there ensued a rumbling as if from the bowels of the earth. The car, nicknamed "Streamliner," was a 560-horse monster machine with a top speed of more than 300 mph. Sleek and streamlined in front, the rear swooped up and out to form a boxlike chamber, behind which Howard pedaled his bike. From the side it looked like a torpedo with exaggerated Edsel fins.

Howard tugged on his gloves and helmet, then straddled his $10,000 custom-made Pepsi Challenger. Next to the car, the bike appeared tiny and primitive. Howard—a lanky 6'2"—appeared out of place draped over its handlebars, like an adult on a child's bike.

But he was not out of place; he was right where he belonged. And, in his estimation, he was the only one who belonged there, the human being most qualified to attempt to break the speed record. While it was important to Howard that he hold records at both ends of the cycling spectrum—speed and endurance—it was the speed record that truly represented the crystallization of his childhood dreams....

He'd only recently begun to realize it, but he'd been training to break the speed record for 20 years. As a kid, he had practiced drafting behind 16-wheelers while they careened down Highway 38 just outside Springfield. "The first time I ever tried it," he recalls, "a cop pulled me over and gave me hell. It didn't stop me, but it did keep me from doing it downtown in broad daylight."

While other Missouri kids had heroes named Stan Musial or Jim Hart, Johnny Howard used to get starry-eyed over a Frenchman named Alfred LeTourneur. Who? "Alfred LeTourneur was the first human to ever go more than 100 mph on a bicycle," Howard says passionately. "I read about him in a comic book insert. I was fascinated ... I couldn't believe anyone could go that fast."

Imagination captured, Howard proceeded to learn everything he could about the land-speed record. Soon he could recite the list of record holders as glibly as the neighbor kids could the St Louis Cardinals' lineup.

First, there was Charlie "Mile-a-Minute" Murphy, a New York City cop, who was best known for chasing down crooks on his bicycle. Murphy, looking to turn his cycling prowess into a Vaudeville act, laid planks between the tracks of the Long Island Railroad and used the slipstream of a locomotive to cycle one measured mile in 59 seconds.

Then, in 1949, LeTourneur broke the century mark, doing 105 mph behind a quarter-midget race car on the Bakersfield Freeway.

Another obsessed Frenchman, Jose Mafferet, tried for the record, but crashed and nearly died. After two years in the hospital, he came back, with an "if-I-die" note in his pocket, and broke the record: 127 mph behind a Mercedes on the German Autobahn.

In 1973, Dr. Alan Abbott, a physician with an extensive background in motorcycle racing, designed his own bike, modified a 1955 Chevrolet drag racer, took both to Bonneville, and pedaled 138.671 mph. Now Howard intended to add his name to the list of record holders. Already he'd come close: an unofficial 135 mph last year on uneven pavement near Mexicali (they couldn't get on the salt flats because of the heaviest rains in 100 years). Then just yesterday, Vesco had gone 137 mph—but without Howard, who had fallen from the slipstream and was hit with swirling sands that blinded and choked him.

That's what it was all about: finding—and staying within—the perfect slipstream. Without the aid of that placid pocket of thin air that gets sucked along behind large, fast-moving objects, the record for fastest pedal-pusher falls to 62 mph. All other things being equal, Howard, following a swooped-up, souped-up race car, figured to have quite an advantage over Abbott and his 1955 Chevy.

Their bikes were almost identical. Howard had teamed up with Doug Malewicki, the madcap genius who had engineered a car that ran on peanut oil, as well as Evil Knievel's rocket car for the Snake River Canyon jump. Bicycle frame builder Skip Hujsak also joined them. Together, they went to see Abbott, finding him cooperative, even enthusiastic. He allowed them to photograph, measure and test-ride his record-setting bike. The result: The Howard bike was first cousin to the "Abbott". It had heavy, chrome molybdenum tubes gussetted at the stress points, as well as motorcycle forks and wheel rims. The biggest difference was that Howard's bike had double-reduction gearing—two chains, four sprockets—resulting in gearing so low that one turn of the pedal translated into 90 feet of travel; gearing so low that Howard had to be towed up to 60 mph.

An aide hooked the 3-foot tow cable from Vesco's Streamliner to Howard's bicycle. The roar of the car was loud and deep, suggestive of a pride of hungry lions. Howard, bathed in sweat, dropped his helmet visor and flicked a switch on his handlebars that gave him radio contact with Vesco in the car.

"Ready, Rick?"

"Ready, John. You?"

Howard nodded, smiled wanly, and said, "Getting close. Got a feeling."

Nothing more had to be said. He and Vesco were by this time almost telepathic. At first, they'd made a point of sharing each and every new piece of information, no matter how trivial it seemed. After all, Howard's success and safety—while they were zipping along the salt at more than two miles-per-minute— depended on their staying in perfect tandem at all times.

Howard sat on his bike staring into the box. The upper part of that aerodynamic structure had a Plexiglass window, through which Howard could see the salty track shimmering ahead. Just below the window, orange letters read: "FASTER, YOU FOOL !"

Car and driver would have about three miles to get up speed. Then they would enter the timed mile, a surveyed section marked by electronic eyes. After the second light, they'd have about a mile to slow down and stop, which often was the toughest part of all.

Howard gave the high sign and they began to move, Vesco accelerating slowly, smoothly, pulling Howard behind him. Although John could have pedaled from zero-to-sixty under his own power, the effort would have left him exhausted for the high-speed struggle ahead.

As their speed increased, it became crucial that Howard keep the front wheel of the bicycle within an invisible 10-inch pocket. If he went too fast, he'd crash into the bumper-bar of the car; too slow, he'd fall from the slipstream, subjecting himself to the swirling turbulence of hurricane winds.

Even the slipstream itself, Howard reminded people, was not a void or vacuum, not a downhill coast. Above 90 mph, there was "an incredibly powerful vortex of air pushing at you."

30 ... 40 ... 50 ... Thus far the ride was smooth, and Howard could still read his speedometer. A wave of exhilaration washed over him. He sensed it all coming together. His body felt good, the bike felt fine, he and Vesco were in sync ... what could go wrong?

The night before, while he and his entourage were camped around a fire on the salt flats, one of the motorcycle types hanging out with them had asked John, wasn't he disappointed that he hadn't broken the record the first day out?

"No," he'd replied evenly, "we're here as long as it takes. It's all coming together. You need the speed to come in small doses so you can get used to it, so you can predict what's going to happen."

Someone laughed. "At 130 miles-per-hour, how can you predict anything?"

"One-fifty-two," Howard corrected. He'd been visualizing that number for weeks; it was now indelibly imprinted in his mind.

"Why take such risks?" someone else asked.

It was Howard's turn to laugh. "It's a risk all right, but a calculated one."

It was a distinction he believed in. In the more than two years since he had begun to openly challenge the speed record, he had constantly been asked about the "danger" and whether he had a "death wish." Yet, strangely, in the previous 15 years, while he was road-racing all over the globe, danger was rarely mentioned. That in spite of the fact that road racing against others was clearly more dangerous—less "calculated"—than racing against the clock at Bonneville. In road racing, he'd seen maimings, even deaths; and Howard himself had been a narrow escapee more than once.

There was, for example, the trans-Florida race, in which another rider half-wheeled him (his front to Howard's rear), forcing him into the oncoming lane of cars. Suddenly, before he could even be scared, a 16-wheeler roared by, missing him by inches.

In another road race, as he was careening down a serpentine mountain road at about 60 mph, he suddenly spotted out of the corner of his eye a slow-moving truck (the road was supposed to be closed!) coming up the mountain. He feathered the brake and began a semi-controlled drift that brought him nearly parallel to the truck, whereupon he struck its flank a glancing blow. He was thrown from his bike, but not far, suffering only bruises and a gash on his leg. The rider on his tail, however, was not as fortunate. He hit the truck straight on, flipping over the handlebars and flying thirty yards into a pile of rocks. As a shaken and battered Howard struggled back on his bicycle (he would finish the race), he could hear the agonized screams of the other rider.

Another time, during a race in Mexico, as he led a pack of riders through a village, a dog ran out onto the road—and stopped! He had time only to silently ask himself, "What do I do now?" when suddenly a Mexican cop pulled out a pistol and shot the dog, which exploded before Howard's eyes.

Fear was no stranger to him; but his greatest fear was that he wouldn't go fast enough. For him, the desire to break the record was a stronger motivator than the fear of getting hurt.

"On another level," he says, "I was afraid that the reporter from *Sports Illustrated* would leave before I could break the record."

55 ... 60 ... Howard released the lever that disengaged the tow-cable. While Vesco continued to accelerate ... 70 ... 80 ... 90, Howard

pedaled harder and faster, trying to maintain a constant distance behind the car. He would later compare the exertion needed during this phase to "riding a kilometer time trial or a 4,000-meter pursuit on the track—although the speed on the salt flats was much more exhilarating.

100 ... 110 ... 120 ... He was caught up in the slipstream now, but staying on Vesco's tail was still a terrible strain on his arms and shoulders. This was cycling all right, but also a bit of tightrope walking. If Vesco veered a few inches, Howard had to be able to adjust instantly. There was nothing in his world but the bike, the salt, and the five square feet of screen in front of his face. All motor functions that weren't needed for the task at hand were shut down. So riveted was his concentration that he didn't notice the razor-sting of salt particles that pelted him.

130 ... 140 ... "The record is ours," Howard thought. But suddenly, a strange sensation! As though the rear wheel were sinking into the salt ... and the front one about to fly into the air! Comprehension lagged behind event as he fell from the slipstream, hitting a wall of wind. A swirling tumult of salt engulfed him; the bike began to fishtail. Using his cycling instincts, moxie, and considerable upper-body strength, he rode it out and brought the bike to a shivering stop.

Vesco and the crew found Howard seated amidst the great salt whiteness, a wide smile on his face. "You just set another world record," he told John, eyeing the bike. "The fastest flat tire on a bicycle. I had you doing one-fifty."

Howard just kept on smiling. Most people suffering a flat tire at a speed faster than the takeoff velocity of a Lear Jet would have given up bicycling for lawn bowling, but not Howard. He was just tickled by the whole thing. The way he figured it, he had just survived the worst they could throw at him. For him, that flat tire was nothing but a confidence booster.

Two tries later, Howard set a new world speed record: 152 mph—the exact figure he had been visualizing for weeks.

"I would have tried another run," he later said, "but by then I'd had a couple glasses of champagne. I didn't want to be unsafe."

Now, two years later, seated in his Encinitas home, Howard proudly speaks of accomplishments, past, present and future. "There's nothing quite so impressive to me as plain, old gut-wrenching determination. I enjoy going out there and finding out just how much self-determination I have stored in me. The thing most people have never learned is how to suffer, how to push back their pain. The feeling of self-accomplishment after having done just that—it's a high you won't experience any other way. I find that surprisingly few people know what that's about. You have to do it until it hurts, then keep doing it until the hurt is part of you."

That's just the way Howard talks: direct, honest, forceful, with a sprinkling of arrogance. With his lean, firm jaw and laser blue eyes that seem to look right through you, his manner does not encourage discussion. It seems to say, "This is the way it is; if you don't like it go talk to someone else."

But there is another side of John Howard: a softer, more contemplative side that occasionally reveals itself: "I look upon the land-speed record not so much as an act of daring, but as a learning experience. It helped me learn more about myself and where I want to go.

"I realized when I hadn't broken the record (at Mexicali) that a component was missing. So I sat down with a fitness guru who told me, 'You already have the hard stuff—the physical part—but what about the soft stuff?' So I started meditating on the unsuccessful attempts, trying to see it all correctly coming together. I saw myself— it was either a dream or a meditative state—doing 152 mph. It seems I had programmed my subconscious mind to create my own reality."

Never before had Howard mustered that kind of mental discipline. "Before the speed project, my subconscious mind had never been used for anything but daydreaming. Going for the record helped me focus my energies, helped me gain control of my mind. I programmed it to accept nothing less than the record."

But records are made to be broken and Howard fully expects someone, someday, to break his. In fact, he welcomes it. Those who would try have his blessing, but as he speaks he is aware of only two men—An Aussie and a Brit—who actively pursue the record. Both have called Howard for advice; he gives it freely, but apparently with little effect, for neither has yet come close. "The Brit has bad equipment and the Aussie doesn't have a good place to do it," says Howard. "I'll help them if I can, but they don't seem to have a sense of what it takes. It's a logistical and financial nightmare. To break the record cost $100,000 (most of which came from Wendy's, Pepsi and KHS Bikes) and 2½ years of my life....

"Of course I want someone to break the record. Where's the drama in breaking your own record? I want someone to break it, then I'll come back and put it away for good. I think 200 miles per hour is realistic."

John still remembers the terror he felt when, as a young Olympian, he first spoke at his father's Toastmaster's Club. Now he talks in front of crowds for a living. He's started his own company, called "John Howard Performance," and his job is to travel around the country and give motivation seminars and fitness workshops. He wears a suit and tie and speaks to groups of businessmen and sportsmen on subjects like Motivation In Sport And Life ... Focusing One's Energy ... Developing The Winning Spirit ... In short, the John Howard Performance Technique.

But Howard is much more than Athlete turned Salesman. The man still performs—and performs well. "I've recently won a couple of bike races, which has rekindled my interest in competing," he says.

Actually, Howard's interest in competing needed no kindling. It had not waned, just been rerouted. The ultimate competition—with himself—remains the dominant force in his life. It is evident in his favorite, oft-repeated quote, from Norman Mailer's "The Executioner's Song: "No psychic reward can ever be so powerful as winning a dare with yourself."

He dared himself to go 152 on a bike, took the dare and won. Now he wants someone else to break the record, so he can go out and do it again. But he is not sitting home waiting for the rest of the world to catch up with him. He has other plans. "The Daedalus Project," he says. "In Greek mythology, Daedalus, the father of Icarus, was victimized by King Minos of Crete and forced to flee—by air! Everybody's heard of Icarus, who flew too close to the sun and melted his wings. But Daedalus was the real hero—he made it, 69 miles to the Greek mainland."

Who is this Daedalus and what is he to John Howard? It seems that some M.I.T. scientists have designed a 68-pound pedal-powered airplane, with 104-foot wings and an 11-foot propeller, and they need someone to pedal it from Crete to Athens—the same course Daedalus flew.

John Howard, of course, wants to be the one chosen to pilot the craft. A pedaler from way back, he wants the chance to break the world's record for non-stop human-powered flight (presently 22 miles across the English Channel). He knows that the man or woman who does it will have tripled the world's record, possibly the greatest differential ever between best and second-best in a sporting event.

Whoever ultimately pilots the plane will have to maintain a speed of 15–17 knots (15–30 feet above the water), the equivalent of bicycling 23 mph for four hours. For a pedal pusher, it's the endurance feat of the decade. To accomplish it is going to require not only state-of-the-art technology and a world-class athlete, but also a great pilot. Realizing that, Howard is taking flying lessons. "My instructor is an ex-Blue Angel," he says. Then, with characteristic assuredness: "He is to flying what I am to bicycling."

Flight training has led Howard into hang gliding. He recently bought a kite and has begun flying at every opportunity. He is plotting a return to Bonneville and a challenge series with riders like Nakano, the 10-time world sprint champion from Japan. He has started a "School of Champions," which takes him all over the country coaching and training other athletes. Next week he jets off to Hawaii for two weeks of intensive flying lessons; he just got back from Europe. Whether he is running, pedaling or flying, he is a man forever on the move. Not many can keep up with him and that includes the women that have inhabited his life. He has gone through a divorce and another painful, extra-marital breakup. Although he likes his life and claims he wouldn't have done it any other way, he knows he has paid dearly for the privilege of Doing It His Way.

"Obsessive behavior in sports and marriage are not compatible," he confesses. "I was married for several years to a wonderful person, but when given the choice between my marriage and athletics, I chose athletics. . . . You know, traveling was the perfect yardstick for that relationship: The first year, whenever I returned from a race, my wife would meet me at the airport gate; the second year, in the lounge area; the third, outside the terminal; the fourth, she said, 'Why don't you take a cab?' And the fifth it was, 'I don't care if you ever come home.'"

For John Howard, though, it's been a fair trade. "What I like best about my life is it's never boring. There's a real progression.

Even when I'm not improving as an athlete, I'm getting smarter, growing as a person...."

He longs to end the interview. He's been sitting a long time and he's antsy. If he doesn't leave now, he won't get in fifty miles on the bike before dark. He rises, saying, "Someday I'd like to get married again, have kids, live on a farm...."

For anyone else, it's a perfectly ordinary dream.

HOWARD UPDATE: In 1987 more than 50 Olympic Cyclists tested for the Daedalus Project. Four were chosen. John Howard finished fifth. Part of the problem was size. "I was just too damn big to fit in the cockpit," he says. "We are also plotting a return to Bonneville and a challenge series with riders like Nakano, the ten-time world sprint champion from Japan."

SPEED FREAK

"There is no meaning to life except the meaning man gives his life by the unfolding of his powers."
—Erich Fromm

CERVINIA, ITALY, 1974, DAY 1: Two 20-year-old Americans strolled into a small town on the Swiss border. They were there, in the shadow of the Matterhorn, to ski the Kilometer Lanciato, a.k.a. the K.L., the Flying Kilometer, the World Series of Speed Skiing. People stopped and stared, drawn not by their reputations, for they had none, but by their beards, blue jeans and below-shoulder-length blond hair, which contrasted sharply with the trim sartorial elegance of the European racers. The people pointed and called them "hip-pies." After the week of racing was over, they would be calling them "The Yankee Flyers." In their hometown of Squaw Valley, California, they were called Steve McKinney and Tom Simons.

SQUAW VALLEY, CALIFORNIA, 1985: McKinney, his 6′ 2″, 190-pound body sprawled on the couch in his Squaw Valley home, remembers that time. "We lacked the heavy 240-centimeter skis, the sleek aerodynamic helmets and the nonporous skintight rubberized suits employed by world-class speed skiers. We were skiers all right—had been since childhood—but by world-class our specialty was the Downhill, where top speeds were less than 70 miles per hour. Alessandro Casse's world speed record—set at Cervinia—was 114.47 mph.

"When I started skiing, I quickly gravitated toward the fastest downhill courses, then the fastest sections of the fastest downhill courses. But I got impatient with turns; without enough speed I was bored."

He'd come to the right place—there were no turns at Cervinia. The eight-meter-wide track ran straight down the face of a glacier. About 500 meters from the start, the skier passed through an infrared timing light; a hundred meters (and less than two seconds!) later, he passed through a second timing light. If he fell or failed to finish within 5% of the leader's time, he was eliminated. As the days went on, the starting point was moved higher and higher up the mountain.

A speed skiing race consists of three phases: the start, the tuck, the finish.

The start—in both speed and alpine skiing—is the same. From a standstill, the racer first poles, then skates to attain maximum speed quickly.

The tuck is where the race is won or lost. "The chest should be on the knees," says McKinney, "so the wind doesn't hit it and force the body up. The arms are in front, breaking the air for the body. The head is tucked low—but not too low, as the eyes must be able to see. Even though you are traveling fast, the overall effect should be stillness. As an old Zen saying advises, 'Non-action within action.'

"But stopping is the real heavy—especially at Cervinia. The glacier has receded, thus the bottom of the run is very steep, and the transition from 'Go' to 'Stop' is abrupt. It changes from a 67-degree downhill to 15 yards of level to a 12-degree uphill, and has the force of 3G's—three times the force of gravity—a force that," McKinney says, "wants to put you on the tails of your skis."

Or as retired speed skier Dick Dorworth put it: "It's a transition that would like to suck you down, break you into a million pieces and spit you out in China."

CERVINIA, ITALY, 1974, DAY 2: Steve McKinney stood near the top of the run, waiting his turn at the mountain. He was wearing a borrowed red-and-black stretch suit and a borrowed helmet. He was to go third, behind a Finnish boy and a Swiss skier named Jean Marc Beguelin. While he waited, he did breathing exercises and yoga stretches. Nearby, a Japanese skier did Tai Chi while an Italian crossed himself and prayed silently. Whatever works, thought McKinney. Calmness equals emptiness. . . .

A push with the poles, four quick skating steps, and the Finn was off. He immediately dropped into a knee-to-chest tuck, then, so steep was the slope, he disappeared from McKinney's view for most of the run. So steep was the slope, in fact, that if a skier could stand vertically on the run, he would be able to reach out and touch snow. So steep that ordinary people, when first laying eyes on it, invariably mumbled obscenities, then retreated to the nearest bar.

Thus far, for McKinney and Simons, the early runs—70, 80, 90 miles per hour—had been smooth and easy. But today they'd hit 100, and with a low-lying fog to boot.

Beguelin pushed off, dropped into a tuck and disappeared from view. While McKinney, eyes closed, imagined his own perfect run, Beguelin ran into trouble. In a lower tuck than usual, he lost sight of the track, veered blindly off course, crashed into a timing apparatus which nearly ripped him in half, then soared off a cliff and landed on an ice field.

Squaw Valley, California, 1985: "I've often questioned why I wasn't more broken up over Beguelin's death," says McKinney. "Was I that callous a person? No, I think it was a matter of concentration, which is crucial in speed skiing. I had my own task to perform, and only by concentrating on that was I going to be able to prevent the mistakes Beguelin had made. That was the way I viewed it."

Such a view was prerequisite to success. McKinney won the Flying Kilometer (Simons was 2nd) in a time of 117.5 mph, the first of his five world records.

Steve McKinney, it seems, was born to set records. He was raised in the ultimate skiing family—seven kids, seven skiers, though it began at least two generations earlier than that. Steve's mother, Frances, has a photograph of her mother soaring off the ski jump at Lake Placid—in a skirt!

Steve's parents were divorced when he was only five, and Frances raised the seven kids. "A strong woman," he says. "She had very definite ideas about the importance of physical and mental balance for good health. Besides mother and teacher, she was athletic director." The McKinney kids, shuttled between their Kentucky horse farm and Lake Tahoe house, became as proficient on horseback as on skis. Frances turned their Nevada home into a ski school, then pressured the Governor for a license to legalize the fact. Thus, the McKinney home became the Ponderosa Day School.

Steve speaks proudly of his mother: "She was a pioneer. The ski academies, where the students ski half-time, study half-time—she originated that format."

Besides Mom, Steve's three older sisters also loomed large in his development as a skier. His earliest memories were of skijouring, in which one of his sisters rode a horse and towed little Stevie on skis. Despite such familial support, Steve feels he started skiing too late. "I was six," he says, "but Tamara was on skis as soon as she could walk."

Tamara McKinney, Steve's 23 year-old sister, lives in her own wing of the Squaw Valley house. She is an Olympic skier, and the only American woman to win the World Cup. She is an amateur skier who, because of endorsements, makes ten times as much money as her professional brother.

"Yeah, it's funny," says Steve with no trace of bitterness. "I make $20,000-$50,000—if I set a world record—but Tamara makes $200,000 just for being Tamara. She also gets about a hundred times as many fan letters."

Despite their skiing accomplishments, Tamara and Steve agree that the most talented McKinney was sister Sheila. "She was the best of us all," says Steve sadly, "but during a World Cup race she released from her bindings and hit a lift tower. She was in a coma for 18 days. She's doing all right now, but there's still motor problems. She doesn't ski. She could, but she won't do it unless she can do it really well." Steve smiles. "Like all of us in this family."

Steve McKinney grew up fast and hard. When he was 14, he was smoking a little pot and raising a little hell; but he was also well on his way to developing what race doctor Zilioli Lanzini would call "a terrifying physique." While still a teenager, he decided to devote himself to the pursuit of skiing excellence. Or, as he put it, "I cut my hair and began to concentrate on the ski-racing gig." Showing his characteristic drive, he made the U.S. Ski Team by the time he was eighteen.

McKinney and Simons, who was also on the team, skied well enough, but the discipline demanded of potential Olympians chafed them. The coaches drew lines and they regularly crossed them, which qualified them as "discipline problems."

"We couldn't figure out," Simons likes to say, "why we had to have a Marine haircut to race for the U.S."

McKinney was the first to quit. Just before a World Cup race, he packed his backpack and hitched to San Francisco, then caught a boat to Alaska. As he remembers, "I was full of idealistic visions of cabins in the woods and self-sufficiency, but two weeks of rain drove me bats. I began to miss the spring skiing at Squaw Valley and thought, 'What am I doing here?'

"When I got no answer, I returned to California and took up rock climbing."

BLACK WALL, DONNER PASS, CALIFORNIA, 1973: Neophyte climber Steve McKinney shielded his eyes from the granite glare and squinted up at his partner, Craig Calonica, who was perched on a narrow ledge twenty feet above him.

"Hairy and scary," Calonica called down to him, but McKinney was already climbing, pulling himself up the sheer granite rock, his huge hands finding holds where none seemed to exist. What he lacked in technique, he made up for in strength and instinct. He had taken to the sport naturally, perhaps too naturally. . . .

Eight feet from the ledge, he hesitated, reached up, missed and fell. Calonica couldn't believe how fast he dropped—forty feet in an instant, hitting a ledge with a sickening thud, bouncing off, then stopping two feet from another ledge when the rope finally went taut. His back was broken.

So upbeat is McKinney's attitude that he can now speak of The Fall only in positive terms. "My speed-skiing career dates from that accident," he says. "I could walk, but I was encased in a neck-to-crotch body cast. Since I couldn't participate in the U.S. Ski Team's summer training camps, I decided to go to Cervinia, where I'd heard about a race with speeds nearly twice what I was used to."

The Italians had long dominated the Cervinia race, and that year was no exception. McKinney watched Alessandro Casse increase his own unmotorized land-speed record to ll4.47 mph. Of far greater importance to the sport, however, was McKinney himself skiing the Plateau Rosa Glacier—in a body cast!

"The cast taught me proper technique. It held my upper body rigid. I couldn't use it to power me, so I was forced to rely solely on my legs and ski only with my knees—technically perfect. I learned to ski quietly, my body riding smooth and balanced."

The accident, McKinney maintains, affected more than just his skiing. "It altered my personality, my entire approach to life. Breaking my back opened chakras—energy valves in the body. Before that injury I was a very macho kind of guy. But afterwards, I started to develop a softer touch, a sensitivity. I learned finesse. It went way beyond sports."

According to McKinney, speed skiing was one of the original racing modes. "For hundreds of years in Scandinavia they've climbed up hills and speed-skied for the purse or the girl." But the sport didn't reach America until 1880, when Tommy Todd won a race organized by the legendary Snowshoe Thompson in an unbelievable time of 88 mph.

Unbelievable because fifty years later, in 1930, the first internationally recognized world record of 63.3 mph. was established by Guzzi Lantschner at St. Moritz.

After World War II speed skiing became a match-play event between two Italians: Olympic downhill champion, Zeno Colo, and his archrival, Rolando Zanni. By 1947, Colo, helmetless and dressed in a woolen sweater, had improved the record to 99.5 mph.

There the record stood until 1959 when the 100-mph mark was finally broken. Except for a brief period in the 60's when the Japanese did well, it remained an Italian event until 1974 when the Americans came to town.

What's it like to be flashing down an icy ski slope at 120+ mph? The mind gropes for comparisons....

The automobile speed limit is 55 mph.

The fastest speed ever recorded in an Olympic downhill race is 64 mph.

A skydiver free-falls at between 117-125 mph.

Yes, but what's it really like?

"It's more like the peregrine falcon," says McKinney, returning to his couch with a beer. "That's what we're really like, flying down the mountain on a cushion of air. Falcons have been clocked at around 175 mph ... " He smiles devilishly. " ... That's a reasonable goal."

When McKinney talks about speed, his voice rises and he licks his lips as though he can taste the speed. " . . . You push off—skate-skate-skate-skate—then drop into a tight tuck that you have to hold without movement. Even a finger can throw you off. Early on, there's no air resistance, and the normal perceptions are there—the rush of the wind, flags here, rocks there. But then you start going faster—70, 80, 90—and now everything is vibrating. You get above a hundred and it's vibrating very fast! You hit that extreme speed, and boom! Suddenly there is no sound, no vision, no vibration. At the crescendo of speed, there is no thought at all."

His explanation for that phenomenon is a combination of Eastern spiritualism, Western hedonism and Einstein's Theory of Relativity.

"As an object approaches the speed of light," he says, "its internal time clock slows down. An astronaut launched into space will age more slowly than his twin brother back on earth. The same is true for the mind of the speed skier. The faster my body goes, the slower my mind works. It's like that White Light place in the Tibetan Book of the Dead. At high speed your senses blend together. You come from separateness and enter into oneness, oneness with the mountain, your skis, everything. In that place you're fully in the moment. No worries about the past or future, only the Here and Now. Being in those other places saps your energy store."

On another occasion, McKinney said, "Speed—the sensation, not the drug—is very sensual. I'll know it's time to quit when I find myself doing it for some motive other than sensuality. It's a healthy, beautiful way to cleanse my system, to give me a new outlook—like a cold bath."

But what of fear? Isn't it scary skiing that fast? Don't speed skiers worry about dying?"

McKinney laughs defiantly. "Fear is always trying to grab you; when you outwit it on the run, it sure feels good. I'm not going to shelter myself from experiences I should have. Seems to me there's no better example of not being here now than worrying about dying then."

Tom Simons, who is back on the circuit after a 3-year layoff, has said, "I want to live, there's no doubt of that. But without my philosophy of thinking that it's not so bad to die, I couldn't do what I do. Every racer knows his life is on the line."

"That's true," says McKinney "We value our lives. I take every precaution to protect mine—except staying home."

McKinney, rising from the couch to get another beer, adds, "I'm more likely to feel fear after the run. As in, Holy shit, I skied down that!"

(Science supports McKinney's experience. Electrocardiograms have shown that although the racer's heartbeat may soar before and after a race, it drops to a more normal pace during a run.)

The present speed-skiing world-record holder, Franz Weber, has said, "I'm always afraid. Fear dominates this sport. I must constantly strive to overcome fear, to master it."

McKinney, however, gives the impression that he is successful not because he rides roughshod over fear, but because he transforms it, from a negative emotion into a positive one. Through sublimation, he uses fear to shove him faster and faster down the mountain.

"When you feel that fear," McKinney says, "it's an amazing adrenaline rush. And adrenaline is the fight-or-flight drug, isn't it? Well, in speed skiing we have to do both."

At Cervinia in 1975, Italian Pino Meyner won the K.L., and McKinney and Simons finished second and third. The following year Simons won and McKinney finished 2nd. ABC came to Italy to film the event and the ratings were good. But in 1977 the race was canceled at the last minute, which soured the network on further telecasts.

"The reasons for canceling the race were bogus," McKinney says. "The Italian officials told us it was because avalanches had destroyed the course, but the real reason was that the Italians were tired of sponsoring a race in which their countrymen had no chance to win. We started to repair the track ourselves, but the bastards brought in snow cats in the middle of the night and destroyed it for real."

In protest, a small nucleus of the best American and European racers traveled to Portillo, Chile, where they founded a world-class track and organized a race. McKinney won that race, breaking the world record by one kph (although it was never officially recognized), and thus starting a strong populist movement in the sport.

As McKinney says, "The biggest outcome of that canceled race was that the racers finally began to take control of their own destiny. Before, it had been a bunch of old men running the show, saying 'go, go, go', even when conditions were dangerous."

Furthermore, McKinney asserts, the Portillo track is much safer than the one in Cervinia. "The Andes are shaped differently than the Alps. In Chile the steepest part is at the top, gradually flattening below. You don't get the radical compression that exists at the finish of the Cervinia track."

In 1978 the racers' conflicts with the Italian officials intensified. Although the race was run, the atmosphere was tense. Once again McKinney won the K.L., and his time of 198.02 kph was tantalizingly close to the magic 200 mark. He could have run again, but he declined.

I could feel 200 in me," he explains. "But I was damned if I was going to break it in Italy. I told the ski companies, "You want 200? Sponsor our race in Chile and you'll get 200."

So Steve McKinney—the Salesman—convinced the racers, the ski companies, the officials and the Longine timing people to go to Chile. It would have been just another letdown story, except that Steve McKinney—the Skier—was true to his word, breaking 200 kph, speed skiing's equivalent of the four-minute mile.

Like Babe Ruth calling his home-run, or Bill Johnson his gold medal, or Cassius Clay his knockout, McKinney had done what he said he would do. And while the world may not always love the self-possessed winner, it cannot ignore him. The event was front-page news in South America and a big story in Europe, bringing McKinney some fame and money. For the first time in his life he could make a living at his sport.

McKinney's impact on speed skiing has been enormous. Besides racer, salesman and ambassador, he has been equipment designer. He has reshaped the helmet used by world-class speed skiers. "In this sport we need more than just head protection, McKinney explains. "We need aerodynamic advantages. A stabilizing effect at high speeds. I spent a week with an Italian manufacturer, making clay molds, and came up with something between an eagle's head and a trout's head. It works."

McKinney also revolutionized the tuck. "Simons and I discovered that if we stuck our butt up a little, it created the sort of stability that you get from a fastback car. We could catch an air stream that actually pushed us forward. Of course, there's a risk. A headfirst fall is the worst for a skier."

McKinney is thinking of the time a skier named Walter Mussner took just such a fall. He was going over 100 mph, when he tumbled head over skis, leaving sixteen holes in the snow and ripping himself open from mouth to pelvis. He came to a stop at the feet of American speed skier, Dick Dorworth. Mussner was dead and Dorworth never raced again.

McKinney himself has fallen only once. Although he wasn't seriously hurt, he is not likely to forget the experience. "I don't wear gloves—the better to feel my way through the invisible tunnel—and when I fell I instinctively put my hands down in the snow to break my fall. It was like putting them on a hot stove."

A skier who falls at 100+ mph runs another risk as well. His rubberized racing suit can melt from the friction and cauterize a wound, leaving a nasty scar. "Sorta like napalm," says Simons.

A modicum of fame has brought McKinney invitations to several "Survival of the Fittest" competitions. "Everything from white-water swims to repelling off tallis slopes," he says. "The crazy stuff we'll do for money. I usually finish in the middle of the pack, collect my thousand or two, and go home.

"My favorite competition was one called the M.V.P.—Most Versatile Performer. I was up against John Riggins and Steve Grogan and about twenty other guys. We did everything from golf to something called Devil Take The Hindmost. The best part was getting drunk in the bar every night with Riggins. . . ."

McKinney also appeared on the TV quiz program, To Tell The Truth. "The first time, I pretended to be a guy who pirates satellite dishes. I fooled Kitty Carlisle, who, when she picked me, said, 'He just looks like a pirate.' Second time I played myself and fooled nobody." McKinney drains his glass and rises for another. "Which proves, I guess, that I look more like a skier than a pirate, eh?"

Off-camera, McKinney was busy searching for a world-class speed-skiing track in the United States. He skied all over the Rockies, searching for a run with such potential, finally locating one in the remote backcountry near Silverton, Colorado. Once more the salesman, he convinced R. J. Reynolds Tobacco Company to put up the $90,000 needed for avalanche control, and by 1982 a track was established that was among the best in the world. That year at Silverton, Austrian Franz Weber upped the world record to 126 mph; McKinney was second at 125.7.

In 1983 McKinney faced a tough decision: Whether to return to Silverton and attempt to regain his title, or to take advantage of a rare opportunity and join an expedition that was out to summit Mt. Everest without the aid of oxygen. In choosing Everest, he said, "I figured there'd be other chances to break the record, but I wasn't sure I'd have another shot at Everest."

It would seem, from the record, that things could not have turned out worse for McKinney. But his eyes see only silver linings, and he has never regretted his decision.

The Silverton course that year was, in Steve's own words, "faster than shit." Franz Weber shattered the world record with a time of 129.1 mph, and Paul Buschmann was 2nd at 127 mph.

Meanwhile on Everest, the action was a bit slower. McKinney was languishing in his tent, five miles above sea level, waiting out a series of blizzards. "Ten days I spent above 26,000," he says, shaking his head. "It does a number on you. When I can't remember something, I blame it on the oxygen deprivation I suffered."

It was even worse for teammate John Roskelly. McKinney's hopes of being the first American to summit Everest without oxygen were dashed when Roskelly developed cerebral edema. He would have died had McKinney not discovered, encrusted in the ice, a half-filled oxygen canister that had been discarded by a previous expedition. Roskelly lived, but the expedition was forced to retreat.

McKinney returned to Everest in the spring of 1987. He, along with Larry Tudor, who currently holds the hang-gliding distance and altitude records, and a few other adventurers, climbed the Chinese side of Everest. Among the other equipment, they lugged from camp to camp several 60-pound hang gliders. The goals of the expedition were twofold: To reach the summit of Mt. Everest; then to soar from a record altitude down into the windswept valleys of Tibet.

"It was the last and best challenge on Everest," says McKinney, who also produced the event. "The mountain has been climbed from every side, soloed, skied and circumnavigated, but it had never been flown. We flew over the holy Tibetan cities of Xigar and Xigase," McKinney says, and then he smiles. "Can you imagine the looks on the faces of those priests when the gliders went over?"

Unlike many adventurers, McKinney makes no lists of goals. "I don't need one," he says. "They just come to me. Like when I was on Everest for that week . . . I watched a huge Himalayan bird soaring on thermals, rising effortlessly despite the thin air. I knew then that we could do it with gliders.

"There's a 13th-century Tibetan book called 'The Unique Juncture and the Right Circumstance.' That describes it. Have a feeling and react to it. Yeah, the goals just come. . . ."

After McKinney returned from his first trip to Everest, he threw himself back into speed skiing. At Silverton he again finished 2nd to Franz Weber, whose world record now stood at 129.3 mph. (The score in seven meetings: McKinney 5, Weber 2.)

McKinney also resumed his role as speed-skiing ambassador. Anxious to upgrade it from its status as a renegade sport, he founded an amateur race circuit called "Sprint."

"It was a way of legitimizing the sport," he says. "We held clinics and races at ten sites around the U.S. In 10,000 runs, the only injury we had was one broken collarbone. There's a lot of frustrated skiers out there who want to go fast but aren't allowed to. We showed that under controlled conditions it could be done safely. If someone wasn't qualified to move further up the mountain, I pulled 'em. We had young kids, old ladies, even a 75-year-old man. Top speed was 81 mph. . . ."

Eighty-one miles per hour. Fast enough by most standards— except those set by McKinney, who regularly races at speeds half again as fast. What qualities in speed skiing separate the Eighties from the One-Twenties?

"Three things," says McKinney. "First of all, there's the equipment. Races are won by fractions of seconds, so the right skis can make a difference. After Beguelin was killed, a lot of the racers refused to run again, including the world record holder, Allesandro Casse. I figured the best skis had to belong to the record holder, so I asked him if I could borrow them. I won my first K.L. on those. Of course, I would've won anyway. . . .

"Second thing—conditions. The best is an icy crust with just a little melting. . . .Afternoons can be so different from mornings, slow tracks from fast tracks . . . .If the times are under 100, I won't win. . . .

"Third thing—ability. The French have a word for it: 'gleesemont'. . . . gliding ability. That instinct for staying off the edges of your skis and relaxing with it. When you go fast enough, you begin to float on a cushion of air. You actually hydroplane."

That, of course, is not the hard part; the hard part is maintaining control when you return to earth. Which is where the fourth element comes in, the one neglected by McKinney, perhaps because he possesses it in such abundance as to take it for granted. Strength. Tendon strength. Particularly the upper-leg tendon strength necessary to hold the tuck for half a minute. The story is told of a McKinney run a few years ago in which he demonstrated just such strength. As he neared the first timing light, one of his huge heavy skis flew up, causing him to lurch dangerously in the wind. Where others surely would have fallen, McKinney was able to force his errant ski back down to the snow, right himself and finish the race.

CERVINIA, ITALY, 1974, DAY 5: Steve McKinney, outfitted in his borrowed red-and-black racing suit, stood at the top of the glacier, repeatedly checking his equipment, as if his life depended on it. The view was breathtaking—jagged spires, snow-covered peaks—but he hadn't the time to appreciate it. Besides, his breathing was already abnormal. The cold seared his lungs, and the adrenaline pumping through his body caused him to hyperventilate.

Using yoga techniques, he slowed his breathing, then sidestepped into place. The flags that defined the track looked ridiculously close together, and he wondered for a moment if there weren't some mistake.

He secured his helmet, took another deep breath and pushed off—skate-skate-skate-skate—then dropped into a tight tuck. His speed rose above 100 mph . . . 110 . . . 115. . . . To those standing near the track, McKinney looked like a blur and sounded like an atlas missile. To McKinney himself, all was still and quiet. It was a touch of Nirvana.

SQUAW VALLEY, CALIFORNIA, 1985: McKinney, who is currently separated from his wife, sits alone in his darkened living room. While the rest of the household sleeps, he is still alert, fired by a life force that smolders but never dies. Even at 3 a.m. he gives off heat.

The moon rises above the mountains, reflecting light off the snow-flecked granite, bathing Steve in moon strokes. He tries to relax his mind, but it defies him. He thinks of that first K.L. and remembers how nervous he was. Yes, frightened too. Fear keeps creeping in. It wants to subvert the mind, distract it from the task at hand. Mental discipline is the antidote to fear's destructive side. Don't deny the fear. Instead, accept it and focus attention on what's to be done next . . . like his next adventure to the French Alps, where he will once again attempt to break the world record by skiing 130 mph.

What's really inconceivable, he thinks, is that most people live their entire lives as prisoners in their own comfort zones. Nothing risked, nothing lost . . . or gained. . . .

He recalls a line from a book called Inner Skiing: "If we never accept challenges, we are left in the dark about all but our most superficial resources."

McKinney is so nourished by his risk taking, by his frequent confrontations with fear, he wonders: What do other people live on?

Steve Boga was born in Berkeley, California in 1947. He attended the University of California at Berkeley and was graduated with a degree in history in 1969. He has spent most of his adult life teaching, writing, traveling, and umpiring in professional baseball. His articles have appeared in *Referee* and *Sierra Life* magazines.